"In The Still of the Night," 70" x 86"
by Tresa Jones, Seneca, Kan., 2002.

Kansas City Star Quilts

"Season's of the Heart," 45 3/4" x 64 1/4"
by Donna Howard, Watertown, S.D., 2002.

Hearts and Flowers

HEARTS AND FLOWERS

HAND APPLIQUÉ FROM START TO FINISH

BY KATHY DELANEY

Kansas City Star Quilts

Author's Acknowledgements

Even though every book has but one or two authors listed, it is impossible to imagine that the author wrote it alone. I'd like you, the reader, to know all of the people who made this book unique and beautiful.

Thank you to Rich, Sean and Ian Delaney, and to Vi Berry (my family) for your support, patience and encouragement. I really am sorry about the pins!

Thank you to Doug Weaver for giving me the opportunity and to Vicky Frenkel for making such a beautiful design for this book. Thank you, Bill Krzyzanowski, for such wonderful pictures and Leanne Baraban and Jo Ann Groves for all of your help with the how-to pictures.

Thanks to my "Quilt Sisters" (Leanne Baraban – my cheerleader and photographer, Charlotte Gurwell – my quilter and personal inspiration and Linda Potter – my mentor) and to Carol Kirchhoff, owner of Prairie Point Quilts in Shawnee, Kansas, this book was made a dream-come-true.

Thank you to some very good friends and new friends who dropped everything and devoted a great deal of time to making the gallery in this book extra special: Kelly Ashton, Leanne Baraban, Kathy Berner, Dana Davis, Barb Fife, Charlotte Gurwell, Donna Howard, Tresa Jones, Carol Kirchhoff, Linda Mooney, Pat Moore, Nancy Nunn, Judy Oberkrome, Jeanne Poore, Linda Potter, Emily Senuta, Anita White. I am humbled by the encouragement, support and time you freely gave to me.

Thank you to my Beginning Hand Appliqué students who kept asking, "Is that going to be in the book? It should be!" Without you I might have forgotten to include something important!

And last, but by no means least, thank you, reader, for your faith by buying this book. I hope all of your stitches are hidden and that you love, or grow to love, appliqué as much as I do!

Hearts and Flowers
Hand Appliqué from Start to Finish

Author: Kathy Delaney
Editor: Doug Weaver
Design: Vicky Frenkel
Photography: Bill Krzyzanowski
Instructional photographs: Kathy Delaney
          and Leanne Baraban
Antiques in photographs courtesy of Steve Ball,
Horsefeathers Antiques, 913-677-5566,
sball@horsefeathersantiques.com

Published by Kansas City Star Books.
First edition, fifth printing
Library of Congress Control Number:
2002103412
ISBN: 0-9717080-3-7

Printed in the United States of America by Walsworth Publishing Co., Marceline, Mo.

To order copies, call StarInfo at (816) 234-4636 and say "BOOKS."

Or order on-line at www.PickleDish.com.

TABLE OF CONTENTS

Chapter 1   Appliqué Fabrics and More . . . . Page 6

Chapter 2   Preparing the Block . . . . Page 18

Chapter 3   Placing The Appliqué . . . . Page 24

Chapter 4   The Hearts and Flowers Blocks . . . . Page 40

Chapter 5   Putting the Blocks Together . . . . Page 90

Chapter 6   The Gallery . . . . Page 106

Chapter 7   The Star's Index of Patterns . . . . .Page 119

Hearts and Flowers

2

Appliqué is painting with fabric. Your needle and thread become your brush and the fabric your paint. You may create intricate paintings with oils or simple designs with poster paint. Either way, you are painting. Appliqué is the same. You may create intricate flower arrangements or "cookie cutter" shapes. No matter how you do it, appliqué is fun and rewarding.

Hand appliqué is portable and requires few tools. What tools you do use are relatively small. Once you have completed the preparation work, you may put up your feet, relax and stitch!

Appliqué offers many different solutions to many different problems. There is no one way to do anything. I am all about choices when I teach. This book is designed to give you choices to accomplish your best work. I find that each project I do presents itself with another opportunity to use a different technique. I think that the more you know, the easier the technique will be for you. With this knowledge, I hope that you will enjoy doing hand appliqué as much as I do! While I will give you choices, I will also explain how I best like to do any given step.

When I work, I don't wish to do any more than I have to in order to accomplish success. You will never find me basting my seam allowances around a freezer paper form, basting my appliqué to the background and then stitching everything permanently to the background. The way I see it, I've made the quilt three times and I only have one quilt to show for it! If I'm going to make a quilt three times, I want three quilts when I'm done! Therefore, I do needleturn appliqué and make one quilt once. On the occasion of working with very large pieces, I will baste the appliqué to the background for portability. Pin basting is my usual choice, but the larger piece, as in Hawaiian style, affords more opportunity to lose pins that my family tends to find with their bare feet. They are not very sympathetic to my quilt-making endeavors when that happens!

The patterns in this book are designed to take you slowly from being a "beginner" with a simple block to "experienced" with the more complicated "final exam." If you go in order, you'll find that your skills will build until you've finished all 12 blocks. The border will seem almost too easy by the time you are ready for it!

So let's begin at the beginning and make a quilt!

"Hearts and Butterflies," 61" x 75"
by Kathy Delaney, Overland Park, Kan., 2001;
quilted by Charlotte Gurwell, Overland Park.

Hearts and Flowers

Kathy Delaney, with a degree in art education from the University of Arizona, loves to teach. Beginning by teaching art to elementary and high school-aged children, she soon moved on to adults, teaching needle-point and then quilting techniques. She has been work-ing and teaching at Prairie Point Quilts in Shawnee, Kan. since it opened in June 1995.

An award–winning quilter, Kathy's work has been published in several books and magazines.

Raised as an Army Brat, she moved to a new home every year or so. Her final move to Kansas in 1994 let Kathy put down her deepest roots.

Kathy lives in Overland Park, Kan. with her hus-band of 30 years. Together they have two sons, one who plans to make the theater his life's work, and one who plans a career in the United States Army.

Kathy designs patterns for piecing and applique under the name of Fabric Crayon Designs

Hearts and Flowers

Fabrics

In the 1800s many appliqué quilts were done on a solid background. The appliqué was made from prints with patterns and many colors. I think those quilts are much more exciting than the Appliqué quilts made in the early 1900s. Quilters used solid fabrics on muslin. Today, quilters use a variety of fabrics for appliqué, and the designs are especially interesting. Patterned backgrounds as well as patterned appliqué provide all sorts of excitement and interest for the eye.

When I look for fabrics for my appliqué, I look for a "light within." I want a variety of values in a fabric and will avoid fabrics that read as a solid. (Value is light and dark of a color.) Some tone-on-tone prints, while having different values of a color, still read as a solid because the contrast is very low. Low contrast is uninteresting to me. I like to use hand dyes and batiks because they offer such good examples for shading. I've been known to use a strong background if I think it is interesting. I love to hear someone, looking at one of my quilts for the first time, say, "I never would have thought to use that fabric!" I love to include visual surprises. (*1-1, 1-2, 1-3*)

1-1

A note about some of the batiks found at your favorite quilt store: The weave is so tight, many new students to appliqué find batik fabrics to be frustrating to use. When you hand stitch batiks, you will want to use the finest needle you can handle. A #10 may be too thick to easily push through the fabric. Plan to use at least a #11, if not a #12, or you will likely be very frustrated.

I choose fabrics that offer a variety of visual textures created by the prints. I am more likely to use a print that is more random in its spacing than one that reminds me of evenly spaced polka dots. Cotton homespuns can add interest to your appliqué project, too.

Plan to make "Swiss cheese" out of a fabric with a large print motif on a wide background unless you want to use solids in your appliqué. A print full of intricate leaves may be just the perfect fabric for your leaves!

1-2

1-3

NEEDLES

Traditionally, appliqué has been done with a fine needle called a sharp. These needles are longer than a quilting between and offer more control. I found, though, that the sharp was just long enough to dig into the tip of my finger with every stitch. I don't like wearing a thimble so I wasn't happy with this needle. I was introduced to the straw needle and was very happy. The straw needle is longer than the sharp and extends past the tip of my finger. No more sore finger! If you can't find straw needles, look for milliner needles. They are the same thing. I have actually met some very fine appliqué artists who insist the needle to use is the quilting between! Personally, I can't hold one in my fingers! See? There really is no one right way to do appliqué!

The thickness of the shaft of the needle is important to your stitching. The #10 may be easier to thread (larger eye) but the shaft is thicker. The #10 does not bend as easily while you work. The #12 is next to impossible to thread but your stitches will be very fine. The #12 will bend very easily while you work. I prefer the #11 (*1-4*). I can see the eye to thread it. My stitches are very fine. And, while the #11 can bend while I work, I keep using it until I am no longer able to thread it due to the bend not allowing me to reach the eye. If you get used to the #11 and then pick up a #10, you'll feel like you're stitching with a railroad spike!

Sharps come in #10, #11 and #12. Milliners / Straws come in #10 and #11 but not # 12. I tend to use the #11 to appliqué and the #10 to hand stitch my bindings on a finished quilt.

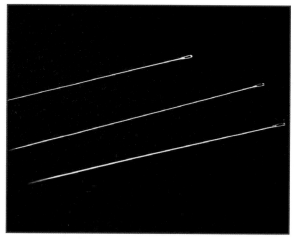

1-4

THREAD

Always match the color of your thread to the appliqué, never to the background.

I find that a regular piecing thread is too thick for appliqué. I want my stitches to be totally invisible. If my thread is thick, it won't hide. So I use a very thin but strong thread. I like Japanese silk the best. Silk thread is so slippery that there is no drag when I'm pulling the thread through the fabric. The color choices are limited but what colors there are seem to be my favorites. I don't have too much trouble finding just the right color. Sometimes a student will complain that the end of the silk thread frays while she is stitching. I'm not sure where the problem is. The end is never used anyway, so I am not too concerned with that aspect. If I find that the end has frayed more than 1/8 of an inch, however, I will snip the end off. Sometimes the frayed end will catch on the thread as it pulls through the fabric and create a tiny knot. It doesn't happen too often, but when I see the end fraying I snip the end.

1-5

If I am unable to find the color I need in silk, I look to fine machine embroidery cotton thread, 50 weight. I find that the colors of the cotton threads are different than the silk threads. Between the two, I have no trouble finding everything I need. These threads are most likely sold at stores that sell sewing machines with embroidery capabilities, if not your favorite quilting supply store (*1-5*).

My philosophy is: The finer the needle, the finer the thread, the finer the stitch.

SCISSORS

Scissors are very important to the appliqué process. There are so many different types and makes. Where to begin? I know that good scissors are expensive. So, I suggest that you begin with one pair, the absolutely best you can afford, and build your collection as you can. I actually use four different pair of scissors. I could get by with one, but work best with at least two.

The most important pair I own are 4" embroidery scissors. These scissors have very sharp points. Without them I could not accomplish the very sharp appliqué points as well as I do. (See Page 33.)

The second most important pair I own are 4" knife-edge embroidery scissors. These scissors are just the same size as the emb-roidery scissors; however, they have one very sharp point and one blunt. Without these scissors, I could have a disaster when I cut the background away from behind my appliqué. (See the chapter entitled, "Finishing.") Both of these scissors come with a choice of regular sized finger holes or oversized finger holes.

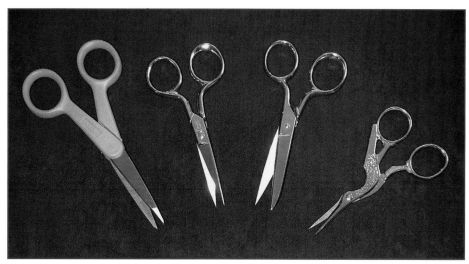

The third pair I use regularly are a medium priced pair with sharp points and plastic handles. The blades are much too thick to accomplish excellent points, but they are perfect for cutting the seam allowances around my appliqué pieces. (See Page 99.) Either of the first two pair of scissors will work here, as well.

The fourth pair I use are the really cute Stork styled scissors. While the points are sharp, the blades are too thick for my perfect points. They are cute, though, so I had to have them to cut my thread. That's all they are made for anyway. As you can see, any of the other three pair will accomplish this feat, but they are so cute! (*1-6, scissors from left: utility, 4" embroidery, 4" knife-edge, and stork*)

PINS

Since I pin baste my pieces as I am stitching to the background, pins are important. Too long pins will get in the way and catch my thread while I'm stitching. So I recommend 3/4" sequin pins or appliqué pins. If you insist on using your glass-head quilters' pins, be sure to pin from the wrong side of the background so that your thread doesn't get caught on the pins. (*1-7*)

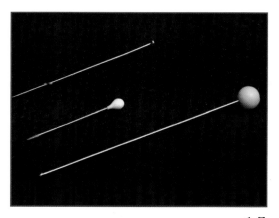

TEMPLATE MATERIALS

There are actual appliqué artists who cut, free hand, fabric for their appliqué and then just stitch it down to their background. I am just not that "free." I use a template to cut my appliqué fabric and I make sure the template matches the pattern exactly. I use several different materials for my templates, depending on the project. I will tell you about several different template styles, giving you choices for how you want to work.

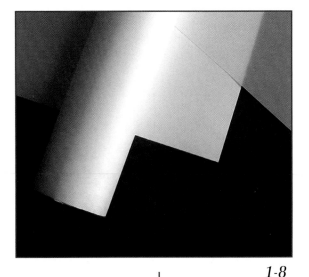

1-8

My template material of choice is most often freezer paper (*1-8, roll at left*). Originally used by homemakers to rewrap the meats they brought home from the grocery before placing in the freezer, this paper has become a staple in most quilters' sewing rooms. I'm not sure how many people still use this paper for its originally intended use, but there sure is a lot of it sold!

Freezer paper is a paper that is plastic coated on one side. The plastic coated side, when pressed to fabric with a dry, hot iron, will adhere to the surface of the fabric until you want to release it. Never use steam, as it will distort the paper. And don't use the hottest setting. I tend to keep the setting at about "wool." The plastic only needs to melt a little to adhere to the fabric. Too hot and more of the plastic melts right down between the fibers and is much more difficult to release.

The template may be reused several times. (I have been told that you can reuse it seven times. However, I used one template on 20 flannel blocks and it was still ready for more!) You should be able to find freezer paper in your grocery store. You will find it with all the foil and waxed papers or you may find it with the canning and freezing supplies. Many quilt stores also carry a type of freezer paper, some printed with a grid on the non-waxed side.

Many quilters choose template plastic to make their templates (*1-8, right*). This translucent plastic is readily available in quilt shops and easy to handle. Templates made from this material can be used over and over, indefinitely.

One can often find, in an office supply store, full-page, self-sticking labels (*1-8, center*). This material can be put through a copy machine or the computer printer to transfer a pattern. The template is cut to shape with household scissors, peeled from its backing and placed on the appliqué fabric. It, too, can be reused. Storage of templates, once used, can be a bit of a problem, as they must be placed onto something that will easily release them for the next use, such as waxed paper.

The sticky paper that is used to line drawers and shelves can also be used as template material. There is a translucent sample that will allow one to trace the pattern. Because the material is less likely to tear in use, it may be used longer than the full-page label.

And last, but not least, you might consider covering your pattern with a laminating sheet, again found in an office supply store, and cut apart. The patterns are reusable and sturdy.

Whatever material you choose for your templates, I recommend that you trace the design as a whole and cut the individual parts apart. The pieces that fit right next to each other share a common line. When you cut this line for both pieces at once, you are sure the pieces fit. If you trace the pieces individually and then cut them out of the template material, you will more than likely find that you have "gaps" between the pieces!

MARKING PENCILS

I feel much more secure if I trace around my template onto my appliqué fabric. (See Page 21.) The appliqué fabric color and value will determine which marker I use. There are many different markers found at quilt stores, some that are guaranteed to wash out and some that say they will wash out but don't. For this process, it doesn't matter if the marker is permanent. All the marks are made in the seam allowance and should not show when you turn them under!

1-9

I use a light marker on dark fabric and a dark marker on light fabric. I want the point of the marker to be fairly sharp so that the line is thin. However, the width of the line does not matter as it is in the seam allowance and will not show (*1-9*).

Some appliqué artists who use the sticky paper (shelf liner or full-page labels), or even freezer paper will leave the template on the fabric while they stitch. The edge of the template is their guide and they make no marks. I don't like this method. I found that I could not see where I was stitching as easily and that my stitches were not as invisible. In addition, the freezer paper never stayed in place for me until I was finished stitching the entire shape. For my purposes, invisible stitches are more important to me than the time I save by not tracing my templates before cutting my seam allowance.

SANDPAPER BOARD

When tracing the template onto the appliqué fabric, place a piece of fine sandpaper under the fabric, sanded side against the fabric. The sand grips the fabric and keeps it from sliding on the table surface. Distortion occurs when no sandpaper is used. If you are using freezer paper templates, the paper releases from the fabric without the sandpaper. It can all be a little frustrating!

To make your own sandpaper board, consider gluing the sandpaper to the inside of a manila folder, a piece of foam-core board or a piece of cardboard (*1-10, commercial board, left; sandpaper in folder, right*).

1-10

PLACEMENT METHODS

There are several ways to transfer your design from your pattern to your background. I find that no one way works every time. Each project I do seems to call for a different method. By giving you some choices, you may find the one that works best for you.

Some patterns are very simple: not very many pieces overlap another piece. The accuracy of placement is not very important. You can let your eye guide your placement and you'll probably find success. When this is the case, I simply finger press the center horizontal and vertical axis and the diagonal axis, if needed, and place my appliqué according to the diagram. This usually works best with symmetrical patterns such as the very simple Rose of Sharon block, popular with our grandmothers and great-grandmothers.

When patterns are more intricate and there are more pieces that overlap to create the design and placement is critical, one of the following two methods might work best for you.

MARKING THE BACKGROUND

Sometimes marking the design directly onto the background fabric is beneficial. Just remember to use a light touch when marking, as you don't want those lines to show when you've finished the appliqué.

By placing your pattern on the top of a light table or against a clean window on a sunny day, and then centering your background fabric over the pattern and securing it, you can successfully trace the pattern lightly onto the background.

Some quilters will use a blue washout marker to trace the pattern. I'm not totally in favor of that particular marker. I've heard of too many quilters who, while they applied water to the marks and made the marks disappear, didn't get all of the chemical out of the fabric before pressing with an iron, setting the marks for good. One might argue that the appliqué should cover the marks anyway, and they should not show. True, but if the chemical isn't totally washed out, it can bleed onto the appliqué and then the iron will set it permanently. Besides that little problem, on a good humid day, the marks can disappear before you have a chance to finish the work. While you can't see it, the chemical is still very much present, again, to be set permanently with your iron. I very rarely use the washout markers.

On a light background, I prefer to use a greaseless, dustless, mechanical pencil. The lead maintains a point, so the line that I make will not be too thick. A really thin line is much easier to cover with my appliqué. I can be relatively certain that my marks won't show once I've completed the block.

On a dark background, I won't mark the design. It really is very difficult to see the pattern through the dark fabric. I will use an alternative method to place my appliqué: a placement overlay.

A simple light table may be purchased at your favorite quilting supply store. You will have to obtain a light to place beneath from a hardware or lighting store. I have just used the fluorescent light that one purchases to place under the kitchen cabinets for extra light in the kitchen (*1-11*).

1-11

A light table can be constructed by placing a piece of glass or Plexiglas on the opening left when removing the leaf from your dining room table. Place a lamp on the floor below for your light source.

PLACEMENT OVERLAY

My favorite method for placing my appliqué pieces onto the background is to use an overlay. This is a transparent or semi-transparent material that has the design traced onto it. This allows me to slide my appliqué piece between the background and the overlay, and line up my piece with the pattern. I have no marks that I have to cover or wash out or worry will show up later.

My favorite overlay material is a clear upholstery vinyl. Upholstery vinyl is usually found in the home decorating department of most fabric stores. I pay about $2.79 for a yard that is about 60 inches wide. There is vinyl that costs about $1.89 a yard, but it is so thin that it tends to stretch very easily. The vinyl that costs about $4.59 a yard is too thick and I just don't need to spend that much! While these prices will not necessarily reflect your market, the important thing to note is that you don't have to pay for the heaviest vinyl, and the least expensive may be too flimsy.

I trace the pattern onto the vinyl with a fine-point permanent marker, making sure that I include any center and side-center markings (*1-12*). The marker point is not so fine, though, that the ink beads on the vinyl. The marker is permanent. That is, it won't rub off. However, the marks will transfer to another part of the vinyl unless you take steps to protect the marks from touching vinyl.

Be sure that you save the tissue paper that comes with the vinyl or use paper towels to cover the side of the vinyl on which you mark. With the paper in place, you may fold the vinyl or roll it for storage and the marks will not smudge or transfer.

I have seen quilters use a thin non-woven interfacing material on which they traced the pattern. They sew this material to the top edge of their background fabric. Each time they slide a piece of appliqué fabric between the overlay and background, they are able to eliminate the step of lining up the overlay to the background. I will say that this method of overlay, while it does eliminate the marks on the background fabric, does provide quite a bit of bulk to handle while stitching. In addition, sliding the

appliqué pieces between the overlay and background can be more difficult. Since the interfacing material has a bit of texture, there is more drag when trying to slide the appliqué pieces and you may end up struggling some to get everything placed just exactly where you want it.

I have been known to use the light table method and not mark my background with the pattern. I simply lay the background over the pattern and place the appliqué pieces directly where they belong, aligning them as closely as possible. I pin baste in the seam allowances and then thread-baste, removing the pins, for portability. I use a contrasting thread, not my appliqué silk and cotton but something I've had forever that did not cost much, and baste inside the turn–under line no closer than the width of the seam allowance that I've cut.

Now that you have all of your supplies in place, let's begin making our quilt!

1-12

Hearts and Flowers

From your background fabric, cut your background block. I always cut the background an inch, all the way around, larger than the finished appliquéd block will be. If, while I am stitching, I am stressed or angry, my stitches will most likely be pulled a little tighter. The next time I pick up the block to work, I might be calm and happy and my stitches won't be as tight. All the fluctuation in the tension in my work can distort the block. When I am finished stitching the block, I press the block and then trim to square it up. If I don't allow extra fabric when I first cut the background, I won't be able to trim the edges to make the block square.

To begin with, I fold my fabric in half and finger press. Don't iron in the crease, you'll never be able to remove it. Open the block, turn and fold in half in the other direction. You should have divided your block into four quadrants (*2-1*). These will line up with the center and side-center markings on your pattern. If there are diagonal markings on the pattern, be sure to fold and finger press your fabric accordingly. These "markings" on your background fabric are especially important if you are using the clear upholstery vinyl overlay.

PREPARE THE OVERLAY (or trace the pattern on to your background)

As I described earlier, I prefer the clear upholstery vinyl overlay for my placement guide. Using my fine-point permanent marker, I trace the pattern onto a square of vinyl, making sure that I transfer all of the center and side-center markings. I don't bother with the stitching sequence numbers, but that is personal preference. (Did I say I don't want to do any more than I have to?)

If the pattern that I am using is a symmetrical design where the whole block is divided into four equal parts that are all the same, I will only trace 1/4 of the pattern. When I am stitching, I can rotate the overlay around the center. Since all four quadrants are the same, placement will be the same. Likewise, if the pattern is symmetrical and divided into two equal parts, I will only trace 1/2 the pattern. Again, when I'm stitching, I can rotate the overlay around the center.

If the pattern that I am using is a symmetrical design where the whole block is divided into two equal parts that are mirror images of each other, I will only trace 1/2 of the pattern. When I am stitching,

I can flip the overlay over the center. Since the vinyl is clear, I can see through the vinyl for placement.

May I suggest that when you trace your pattern, you write the name of the pattern in one of the corners? Don't just mark the top with a "T." Because the vinyl is transparent, the lines that you draw on look the same on the front and the back. It may be difficult to tell which is the front. Trust me, it is very irritating to place your appliqué backwards before realizing what you have done, only to be forced to unstitch and start over. Any of the blocks in this book that begin with 1/4" bias tape stems can get you into trouble. Placing some sort of writing on the overlay to clue you to the correct side will, indeed, save you some frustration.

2-1

The patterns in this book are neither symmetrical nor mirror images, though. You will need to trace the whole pattern.

When you purchase your vinyl, it should come with an equal amount of tissue or liner paper. Don't throw this away. Use it to store your overlays. While the permanent marker will not smudge or smear if you rub the lines you have drawn, they will transfer to another part of the vinyl if you roll it or fold it onto itself. By covering the side of the vinyl on which you have drawn the pattern before rolling or folding, you will prevent your lines from transferring and causing a mess for you later.

If you don't want to use the over-lay method for placement, lightly draw the design onto the background square so you know where to place your appliqué. I try to trace just inside the line on the pattern so that it is just a line's width smaller than the templates I've drawn. When I stitch my appliqué pieces to the background I should be covering the lines on the background. I really don't want them to show.

PREPARE THE TEMPLATES

Having decided which material you will use for your templates, trace your complete pattern. I am happiest using a pattern that includes a full-sized picture of the block. I use that picture to trace my templates. Sometimes a pattern will show a "thumbnail sketch" of the block and provide full-sized individual templates for you to trace. Since we aren't machines that can stamp out the drawing and die cut the shape, each of us will provide a personal spin onto the template. We may add to the curve or flatten it out just a bit. A point may shift just a bit or become a little rounded, a tight curve may become a point. However careful we try to be, we can't help but change something. Add to that the various levels of our scissor cutting skills and we've altered the template again. When we put the templates all together as a puzzle might be, we find that there are often gaps between pieces. No matter how hard we try, we cannot add fabric once we've cut it away!

Because of what I've just described, I prefer to begin with the full sized pattern. I trace the pattern as a whole onto my template material and then, when I cut the pieces apart, any alterations that I make to the one shape are automatically transferred to the adjacent shape. This way I have no gaps. The Quilt Police will not pick up my "alterations."

As with any "rule" there are exceptions. Let's say that my pattern is of a flower arrangement in a vase. Peeking out from behind several stems and extending above that drooping tulip on the left is a long leaf. If I trace the pattern as I have described, I will end up with several templates for that one leaf. Instead, I will trace the leaf separately from the rest of the design and make just the one template for the whole leaf. In appliquéing the stems and flowers after stitching the leaf, I will accomplish the look I desire without so much work.

When I trace my pattern onto my template material, I extend intersecting lines. This means that if a line ends at another line, I will continue the line through. When I cut the parts away from each other, those little marks will be there and aid me in placement when I put it all back together (*2-2*).

2-2

Be sure to transfer the numbers that you find on the pattern onto your templates. The numbers represent the stitching sequence. The pattern has been numbered so that you will begin stitching the piece closest to the background; in other words you stitch first what is farthest away. You build forward. The pieces that overlap need to be placed so that the one behind is stitched before the one in front.

No matter what template material I've chosen, I prefer to trace the "big picture" and extend the intersecting lines. If using freezer paper, trace your pattern onto the paper side. If using the full-page labels or the shelf lining sticky paper, trace your pattern onto the paper itself. Tracing on the backing of either paper or the shiny side of the freezer paper will reverse the whole pattern. If you have decided to make a mirror image of the pattern, don't forget to place your numbers on the "right" side so that you can see them when the backing is removed or the freezer paper is ironed onto the fabric.

Once you have prepared the templates, you are ready to start working with the fabric. No matter what you've chosen for your template material, you will be working with the right side of your fabric. Tracing around the template plastic, ironing on the freezer paper, sticking the full-page label or the shelf lining paper onto the fabric is ALL done on the right side.

A rule that I follow is to always place my template on the fabric so that the majority of edges will fall on the bias of my fabric. It is so much easier to turn a bias seam allowance than one that is on the straight of grain. If you choose a directional fabric for a particular appliqué piece, keep in mind the bias edge rule. Will the pattern still look good? It is not as important that the grain of your appliqué match the grain of your background. However, if you are making what will become your "Master Quilt" and you wish to make sure that it is technically flawless, you might consider making sure that the grain of the appliqué fabric is exactly the same as that of your background.

If you are using the template plastic for your templates, there is no question that you are going to trace around the template. Place the fabric, right side up, on your sandpaper board and trace around the shape. Use a light marker for dark fabrics and a dark marker for light fabrics. (See Page 13.) The line itself is actually going to be turned under when you stitch, so it will not show. If you make a thin line or a thick line, it won't matter. If you choose, you may even use a permanent marking pen, but consider the weight of the fabric. Will your mark shadow through to the top and show?

2-3

If you are using the freezer paper, the full-page label or the sticky self-lining paper, you may decide not to trace the template onto your fabric. Some appliqué artists prefer to save that step. They simply adhere the template to the fabric and use the edge of the template as their guide to turn under the seam allowance. I tried the method but found that my stitches didn't turn out as well. Often, the edge of the template blocked my view of my folded edge and the shape just wasn't done as well as I wanted. My stitches showed, the curves were choppy and I wasn't happy. Since my preferred template material is freezer paper, I also discovered that as I stitched, the paper loosened from my appliqué fabric and I lost the accuracy of my shape. I just think I have more control over my work if I trace the template onto the fabric and then remove the template.

Tracing the freezer paper templates, the full-page label and the sticky lining paper presented a whole new challenge. Our traditional way of tracing is to hold the template with one hand and press the marker against the edge of the template while tracing around. This method tends to lift the paper template from the surface of the fabric with the point of the marker. This causes yet another alteration of that shape and is not accurate. In addition, the freezer paper tends to lift right off the fabric and becomes very difficult to trace.

2-4

Instead of pressing the marker point up against the edge of the template, hold the marker so that the template is between your hand and the point of the marker. You are tracing over the top of the template and the template is not going to move (*2-3*). Your appliqué piece stays the correct size, you have a crisp turn–under line and the shape stays accurate. This method doesn't work as well with the template plastic because the thickness of the material causes a gap between your drawn line and the template, thus enlarging the shape. Again, you lose your accuracy.

Once you have traced all of your appliqué pieces, you are ready to cut your seam allowances. In appliqué, the scant 1/4" seam allowance is really too much. Too much seam allowance around curves and in points adds bulk and doesn't let you have a smooth finish. If you are very new to appliqué, however, you may find that anything much narrower is a little harder to grab with your needle to turn under. I encourage my students to cut a 3/16" seam allowance. After they get the hang of the needle turn technique, they will often cut the seam allowance 1/8 " (*2-4*).

The seam allowance width depends on the fabric you've chosen, too. If you are using a fabric with a looser weave, you might want to give yourself a little extra seam allowance. The needle turn technique, depending on your skill, may chew up that seam allowance a bit and fray it. Remember, you can always cut away fabric, but you can't add it back.

Once I have trimmed the seam allowance around all of my appliqué pieces, I stack them in order according to the numbers that I transferred from the pattern, starting with No. 1 on top. Do not remove the freezer paper templates from the appliqué pieces until you are ready to stitch. Once I have stacked my pieces, I am ready to begin!

Hearts and Flowers

*B*ecause I have made such a good case for the vinyl overlay method, and since it is my favorite, I'm going to assume that you're going to give it a try. So my directions from here on out will include the use of the vinyl.

You have finger pressed the center axis on your background. You have traced your pattern onto your vinyl and included the center and side center markings. Now, working on a flat surface, lay the vinyl, right side up, on top of your background, also right side up, lining up the center and side center marks with the creases. I use the longer glass-head quilters' pins to pin the vinyl to the fabric around the outside edge. I discovered that if I only use two pins, the vinyl would shift easily. But, if I place a third pin, creating a triangle, the vinyl is less likely to shift. Naturally, I pin away

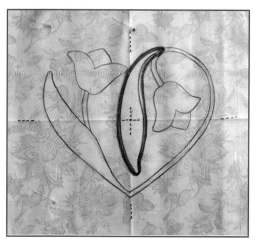

3-1

from where I will be placing my appliqué pieces (*3-1*).

Slightly lifting the vinyl, I am able to easily slide my appliqué piece between the vinyl and the fabric. If I had taken the freezer paper template off before this point, it would have been very difficult for me to slide the piece in. I use the template

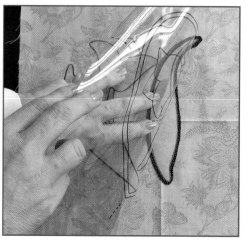

3-2

as a guide. When the template fits within the traced pattern on the vinyl, I let it carefully drop to the fabric below.

Now I am ready to remove the vinyl. If I just lift it, static cling will have caused the appliqué piece to stick to the vinyl so I must be more careful. I hold the vinyl down over the appliqué piece and carefully roll the vinyl away, pulling my hand away at the last moment (*3-2*). The appliqué piece stays where I want it so that I can put

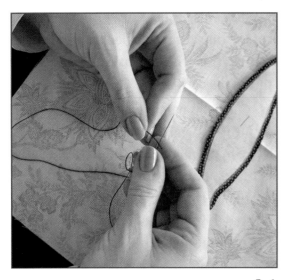

3-4

going to explain it, as I understand the knot. Remember, I'm right handed, so if you're left handed, do what I say, only use your left where I use my right and your right where I use my left.

Once you have threaded your needle and you've determined which end gets knotted, proceed as follows: Hold the needle in your right hand between your thumb and index finger, thumb on top. Lay the end of the thread you want to knot across the needle and secure it with your thumb (3-4). With your left hand, wrap the thread adjacent to the part being held by your thumb around the tip of the needle twice and secure that under your right thumb. At this point, you are holding in your right hand between your thumb and index finger a needle with thread looped around the shaft a couple of times. Continuing to hold the thread that is looped

around the needle, pull the needle out from between your thumb and index finger, without letting go of the thread loop. Keep pulling until the thread has followed the needle and made a pass through the looped thread. When you get to the end, you will have a small knot. That's all there is to it (3-5).

When I was a kid, I was taught to wrap the thread around my index finger and roll the loop off the end of my finger. By holding the little twist of thread and pulling the other end of the thread, I compacted the twisting into a knot. You may be tempted to make this type of knot, but it is too bulky for appliqué. The bulk will show. So, practice until you get this quilter's knot mastered. It is the same knot you use when quilting, as it is small enough to pop through the fabric to get buried in the batting.

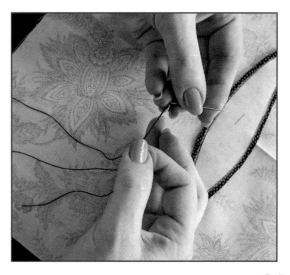

3-5

THE APPLIQUÉ STITCH

With appliqué piece in place and needles threaded and knotted, you are ready to begin stitching. But, where do you begin? Well, that depends on the shape of your appliqué piece.

First rule: Never start at a corner or point.

If another will overlap your shape, begin where the shape begins under the next shape (stitching from right to left over the top if you're right handed; the opposite if you're left handed). Let's take the example of the leaf (appliqué piece #1) in the Tulip Block on Page 45. The base of the stem is overlapped by the flower's stem. As you are looking straight on at the design, you will begin stitching at the upper left corner, stitch around the leaf and end at the upper right corner of the base of the leaf. (Remember that if you're left handed, you'll begin in the upper right and end in the upper left.)

If your shape is going to stand alone or do the overlapping, begin on a relatively straight edge. Take a look at appliqué piece #5 on the Tulip Block, Page 44. I would

begin stitching that flower on the left or right side of the body of the flower. It seems to be the "straightest" of the edges.

Now that you've determined where to begin, let's see how to begin. I begin by bringing my needle from the backside of the appliqué piece, through the turn–under line. This way my knot will be in the fold of the fabric. With the tip of my needle, I prick the seam allowance and then tuck it under the shape, making sure that the turn–under line is also turned under (3-6). I turn under no more than 1/2 " of seam allowance at a time. My left thumbnail is a very important tool to this process. If you bite your nails, OK. But stop biting your thumbnail right now! Right-handers need the left thumbnail and left-handers need the right thumbnail.

3-6

My thumbnail is used to oppose the motion I make with the needle. The needle turns the seam allowance under, but the thumbnail holds the top of the appliqué piece in place so that everything isn't shifted by the needle action. My thumbnail keeps a pretty tight reign on the edge of the appliqué (3-7).

My first stitch is taken into the back-

Once I have my anchor stitch, I turn the appliqué in my hand so that I am ready to stitch up the other side. Using the tip of my needle, I turn under the seam allowance. My first stitch will again be in the inside point. I put my needle into the background under the fold as usual, but this time I go even further so I am right under where the thread is coming out of the top of the appliqué piece, exaggerating this stitch. I travel forward 1/16" and come out in the fold of the appliqué piece. When I pull the thread, I am, in essence, gathering the fabric at the inside point into a tiny bundle. That is what makes the inside point appear sharp and that is what keeps me from having little frayed threads sticking out (*3-17*).

OVERLAPPING
THE APPLIQUÉ PIECES

The first couple of times I taught an appliqué class at my local quilting supply store, I had a couple of students follow my words absolutely to the letter! What I discovered was that there was something I did not say that I took as a given and assumed it was so obvious that everyone else would take them as a given, too. I am very grateful to those students because they helped me become a better teacher.

The extremes that these ladies went to in order that the adjacent appliqué pieces fit together were incredible. They turned under the seam allowances on both appliqué pieces and the work was impeccable! There was no gap and the edges matched beautifully. I did not save them from hours of frustration — but let me save you!

When you have two appliqué pieces that share a common line, as in the Tulips in our Tulip Block, the seam allowance of one appliqué piece does not get turned under, but instead, is covered by the next appliqué piece. The seam allowance of the second piece is turned under and the edge just covers the turn–under line of the first (3-19).

Remember the numbering of the appliqué pieces? Remember that you stitch the piece farthest away onto the background first? If the edge is adjacent to another piece, don't stitch it. It will be secured when the next piece is placed over and the second piece will hide the seam allowance. If you want to, you may stitch in the seam allowance with

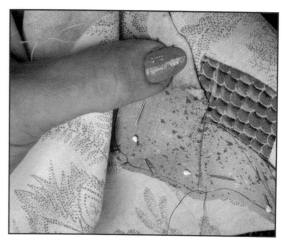

3-19

a small running stitch as you travel to the next part of the seam allowance that does get turned under.

PIECING THE APPLIQUÉ UNIT

When you finish your quilt top, more than likely you will be hand quilting your beautiful quilt. You will want to do the best job possible. After all, you've done a lot of work already, you'll want as perfect a quilting stitch as you are capable of making. From experience, you've probably already discovered that the fewer layers of fabric your needle penetrates, the better your stitch will be. That's why when you quilt a pieced top, you quilt 1/4" away from the seam so as to miss the seam allowance.

One way to aid your quilting stitch is to eliminate layers of fabric where possible. This is especially easy to do behind the appliqué by cutting away the background

3-21

fabric. You only need 1/4" inside the appliqué as seam allowance. The rest can be removed. (See Page 99.)

So that I can remove all of the background behind my appliqué, I often piece a unit before stitching it to the background. I treat the first appliqué piece as the background to the next and so on. The seam allowance that is overlapped by the subsequent piece is left untrimmed until after I stitch so that I have something to hold while stitching (*3-20*). Depen-ding on how many "layers," I may not pre-trim any of the seam allowances except the last piece until after each appliqué piece is added (*3-21*).

Once the unit is pieced, I then stitch it to my background. When I remove the background from behind, I get it all so that when I quilt, I am only stitching through one layer on top of my batting and backing.

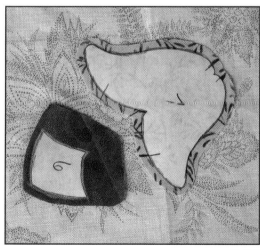

3-20

Hearts and Flowers

The next section of this book will be the individual blocks. Each block has a technique of appliqué that is in addition to all that I've told you about so far. I hope you enjoy making these blocks as much as I did.

Fabric Requirements for my quilt
> (about 61" x 75")

Block background and sashing:
> 2 1/8 yards

Border: 2 1/3 yards
Block frame: 5/8 yard
Border Bias appliqué: 1 yard
Binding accent: 1/4 yard
Binding: 5/8 yard
Backing: 4 1/2 yards

Appliqué hearts and flowers:
You will want to have a large variety of fabrics, but you will need only small amounts of each one. I suggest that you choose your appliqué fabrics as you need them instead of trying to purchase everything at once. You may find that you have plenty in your stash to get started. Refer to Page 7 for ideas regarding choosing your appliqué fabrics.

To determine the amount of fabric you'll need for any given appliqué piece, place a square ruler over the pattern for the piece in question, placing the ruler so that the edges of the appliqué will be on the "bias." (Let the markings on the ruler act as the straight of grain.) Be sure to allow for plenty of seam allowance. The ruler will tell you what size square or rectangle you will need for that particular piece.

Cutting instructions
- From background
  > For blocks - (12) 13 1/2" squares
  > For sashing - (6) 3" x 45" strips
  > (selvage to selvage)
  > From strips cut (8) 3" x 13 1/2" rectangles and (3) 3" x 44 1/2" strips
- From block frame
  > Cut (12) 1" x 44" strips
  > (selvage to selvage)
  > From each strip cut (1) 1" x 12 1/2" rectangle and (2) 1" x 13 1/2" rectangles
  > From strips cut (8) 3" x 13 1/2" rectangles and (3) 3" x 44 1/2 " strips
  > Cut (4) 1" x 44" strips (selvage to selvage)
  > From each strip, cut (3) 1" x 12 1/2" rectangle
- From border (length of fabric)
  > Cut (4) 8" x 84" strips
- From binding accent
  > Cut (7) 7/8" strips (selvage to selvage)

Hearts and Flowers

CUTAWAY APPLIQUÉ

Sometimes it is much easier to stitch an appliqué piece if you don't cut the seam allowance first. It may be that parts of the piece are thin and so will become unruly and hard to handle. Some Hawaiian appliqué designs are like that. In this block, the appliqué piece #3 would be much harder to stitch if you cut the seam allowance first. Instead, trace the template on the right side of your fabric. Notice that if you place the template in the straight of grain, the edges are all on the bias.

I placed my fabric, using the vinyl overlay for placement, and pinned in the direction that I was going to stitch. But, since the stem is pretty thin, I had to pin outside the turn–under line.

Because you are using a template for the stem and not stretching either edge to make the curve, you do not have to stitch the inside curve first.

However, coincidentally, you will be. Using your 4"

embroidery scissors, cut away about 2" of seam allowance. At this point, I like to switch to my 4" knife-edge scissors and I cut with the blunt edge against my background. These scissors prevent me from cutting my background fabric accidentally. In this case, you will need to clip the seam allowance on the inside curves.

Begin your stitching on the right side of the stem at appliqué piece #7 (if you are right handed) and stitch all around the piece, ending at the appliqué piece #7 again. If you're left handed, you will work in the opposite direction. As you stitch a little, you cut a little seam allowance, revealing the background as you go (4-1).

I pieced my tulip head units before adding them to the background. When I stitched the units to the background, I still stitched in the sequence of the numbering when I applied the unit to the background. In other words, I stitched the edges of piece #4 to the background and then stitched #5.

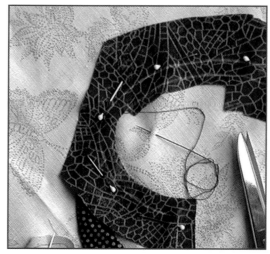

4-1

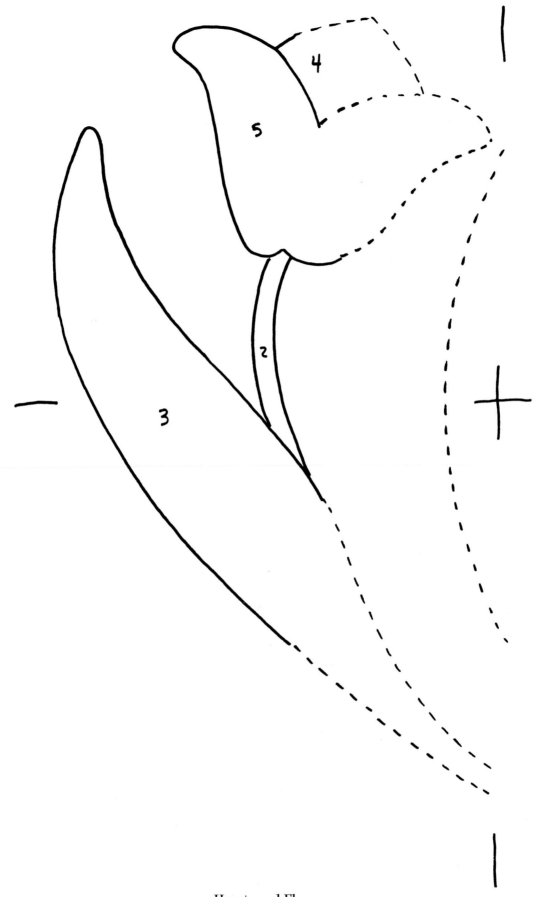

Hearts and Flowers

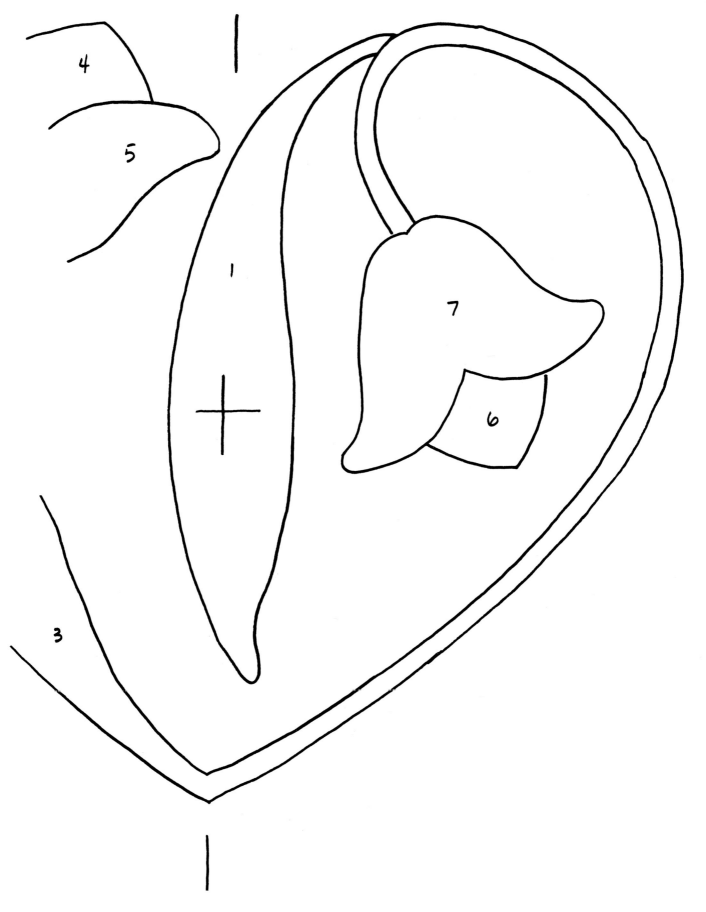

Hearts and Flowers

When tracing my templates, I traced appliqué piece #1 separately from the whole picture. Notice that this leaf is made up of many segments. Not wishing to do more work than necessary, I trace the leaf as if it were one piece. I have included dotted lines to help you determine the shape. Please note that you will not be adding seam allowance to that part of the appliqué piece that is indicated by the dotted line. You will not be turning this part of the appliqué piece under. The numbers in parentheses indicate that while it looks like three segments, it is all one piece.

Where the other pieces overlap, I do not turn under the seam allowance on appliqué piece #1. So be sure that you extend all of the intersecting lines and transfer those lines to the seam allowance. I make a clip in the seam allowance just past the intersecting line so that the seam allowance can turn under just past the appliqué piece that will overlap. My clip is in the direction of where the overlapping piece is stitched so that the seam allowance that is under the appliqué piece is totally hid-

den by that piece. I make the clip because I want the seam allowance that is under another appliqué piece to lie flat so that the fold will not show through as a "bump" (4-2).

I used the cutaway appliqué for piece #5. The three leaves may appear to be three different pieces; they really are all one appliqué piece. The area that connects the three leaves together is rather thin. If you cut the seam allowance, you will have a small degree of frustration when you try to place the piece #5 under the vinyl overlay. It really will be quite unruly. However, by leaving the fabric intact, you will find that placement is much easier. Remember, just cut about 2" of seam allowance ahead of where you are stitching. Once you have stitched about 1 1/2", you can cut another 2" of seam allowance. As you get more and more excess fabric flopping in your way, just cut it off and keep on stitching. Eventually, as you get to the end of your stitching of this piece, you will have it all cut away.

4-2

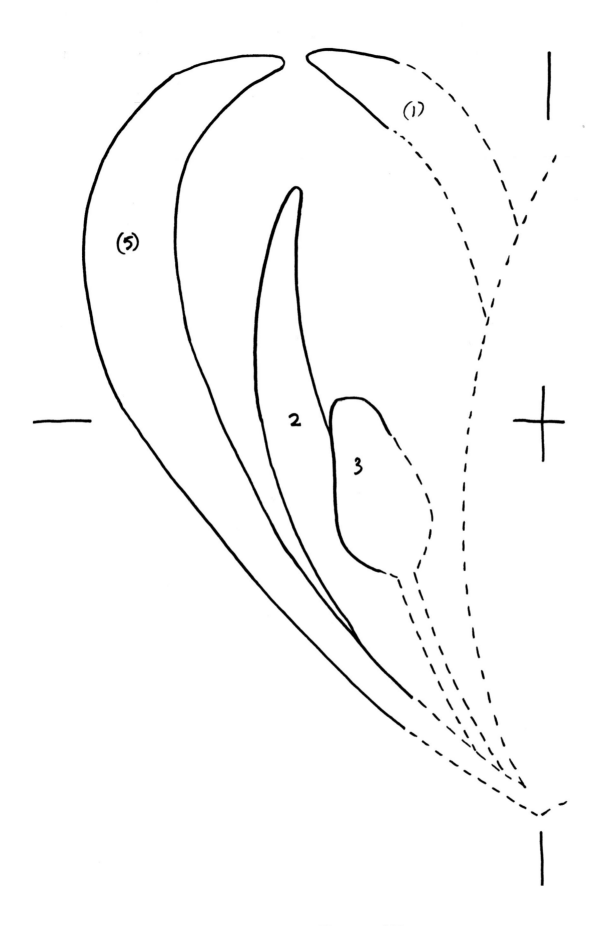

Hearts and Flowers

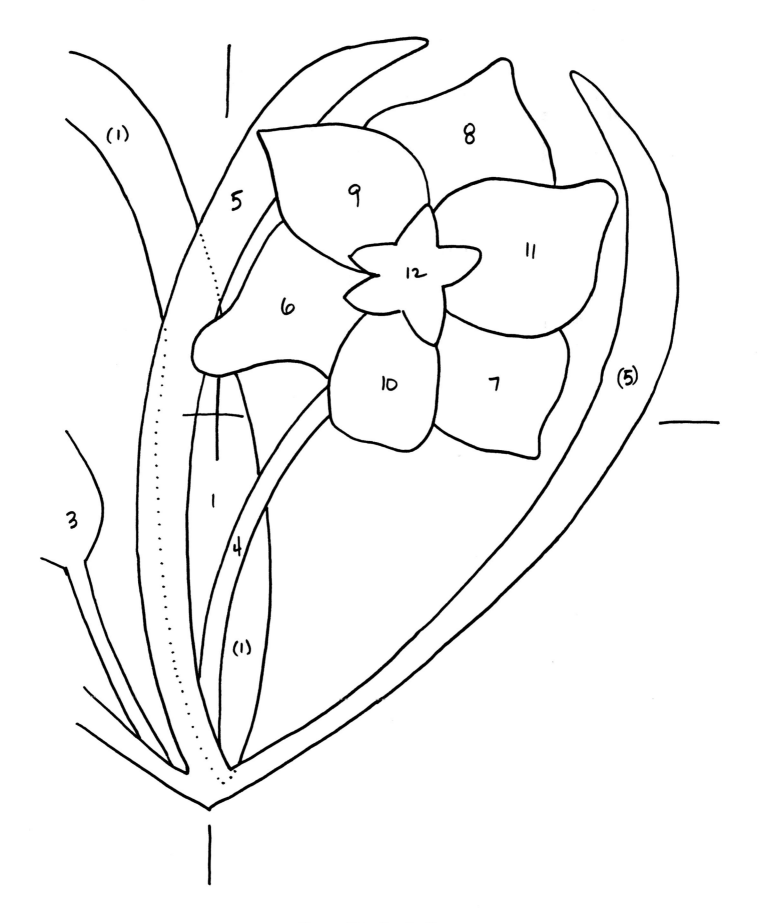

BIAS TAPE MAKER

To make stems for my appliqué, I will often use a bias tape-making tool. I prefer the one that has a plastic insert. The tool without the insert is a single piece of metal and just does not work as well for me with all fabrics. The tool comes in various sizes from 1/4" to 2". I most often use the 1/4" tool and the 1/2" tool. This quilt only requires the 1/4" tool.

4-3

Disregard the instructions that come with the tool. The measurements don't work with our quilting rulers. To make 1/4" bias, cut 1/2" bias strips. Lay a piece of string over the stem pattern and measure. The length of the string will tell you how long a bias strip you will need for any given stem.

Place the 45-degree line on your ruler on the straight edge of your fabric. Cut off the triangle. Using the rotary cutter and the ruler cut the length of bias strips that you need. If your piece of fabric is large or the length needed is more than the 24" length of your ruler, fold a corner up diagonally across to the opposite corner, creating a triangle. Place the ruler on the fabric so that a perpendicular line on the ruler is even with the fold (*4-3*).

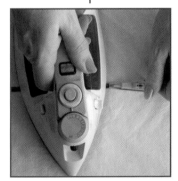

4-4

Follow the instructions for pressing that comes with the tool. There are a few things that I have learned along the way, however, that will not be included in the directions.

1. Your iron must be on the hot and steam setting. Use plenty of steam.

2. This method of making bias strips does not work on a Teflon–covered ironing board cover. If you have one, you will need to work on a different surface. The Teflon doesn't allow the steam to flow through the cover, so you'll burn your fingers. And the fabric won't "stick" to the cover, so your iron will just push it along, not pass over the fabric.

3. Sometimes batik fabrics work and sometimes they don't. I love batik for my appliqué, but can find it frustrating. You may want to wait to use the batiks until after you've gotten used to the process.

4. Sometimes a pin securing the end you begin with may help the process.

5. Pressing the iron down too hard onto the surface causes the bias strip to stretch. Pass the iron over the fabric slowly and lightly.

6. You don't need to hold the tool. Let the side of your iron guide the tool. Instead, use your free hand to guide the fabric. You must feed the fabric into the tool evenly so that the turn under is even on both sides.

7. If for some reason a bias strip gets messed up, you cannot press it flat and start over. Just cut a new strip.

If, as you are pressing, you think you should have kept the iron in place a little longer, you can back the tool up a bit and redo the small section.

8. As soon as you have made a bias strip, gently wrap the bias tape around an empty bathroom tissue or paper towel core and pin. This will keep your seam allowance from relaxing before you have a chance to stitch it down.

I tend to make a bunch of bias tape and then whenever I need some, I'm ready (*4-4*).

Hearts and Flowers

Hearts and Flowers

The tendrils on this block are made with an embroidery stitch called the "stem" stitch after all of the appliqué is done. Begin by placing your block over the pattern on a light box. With a sharp pencil and a light touch, draw the lines. If you aren't heavy handed, your stitching will cover the pencil line. Using a 6" or 8" embroidery hoop, center the area to be embroidered in the hoop and tighten the outer ring.

You will need to experiment to discover the look you like. I use a #7 crewel needle and one strand of embroidery floss. You may wish a heavier line and choose to use two strands. I begin by making a quilter's knot and burying it in the appliqué, pulling the needle out on the right side of the block between the background and the appliqué where the line begins. If you are right handed, you will be working from left to right. Your needle in your right hand will be pointing left. If you are left handed, you will work in the opposite direction but the technique will be the same.

On the line you've drawn, and no more than 1/8th of an inch away from where the thread has come out on top of the block, the needle goes into the fabric and comes up again, still on the line, but half way between where the thread initially came out of the background and where you first went in. When you make this stitch, you want to be sure that your needle does not split the stitch that you've already placed (4-5).

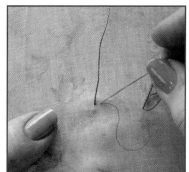

4-5

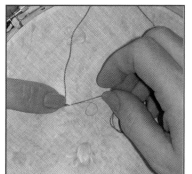

4-6

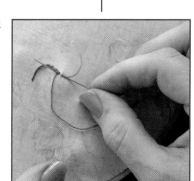

4-7

At this point, you will want to move the thread out of your way.

As I work, my drawn line is horizontal to me. The stitch, when done correctly, will appear to be a tiny "rope." To achieve this look, I use my left thumbnail to hold the last stitch above the drawn line so that when my needle backstitches and comes out on the line in the middle of that stitch, I don't split the thread. When I make the next stitch, the thread looks as if it crosses over the previous stitch. In addition to holding the stitch out of the way, I also keep the majority of my thread out of the way (4-6). Always keep your thread to the outside of a curve. This will help you achieve the "rope" appearance. If the direction of the curve changes, causing you to change the direction of the cross over, then you will need to take one stitch slightly smaller to make the transition. This one stitch will have no crossing–over appearance but because it is so small, it won't affect the continuity of the line of stitching (4-7).

To tie off, I pull my thread to the back of the block and thread the needle through the stitches for about an inch, making sure that I don't catch the background or it will show on the front of the block. When I clip the thread I am reasonably sure that the stitches will stay secure without making any pesky knots to shadow through to the front later.

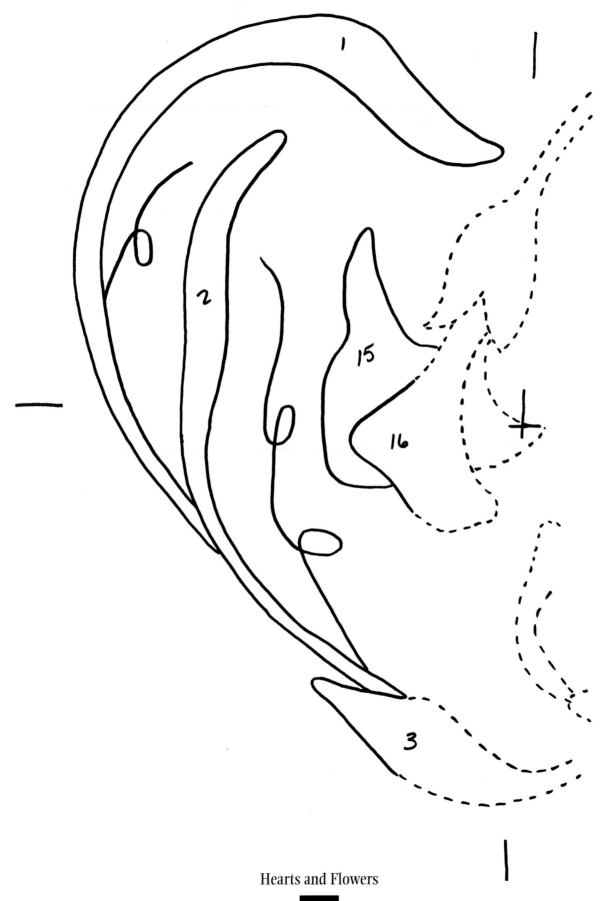

Hearts and Flowers

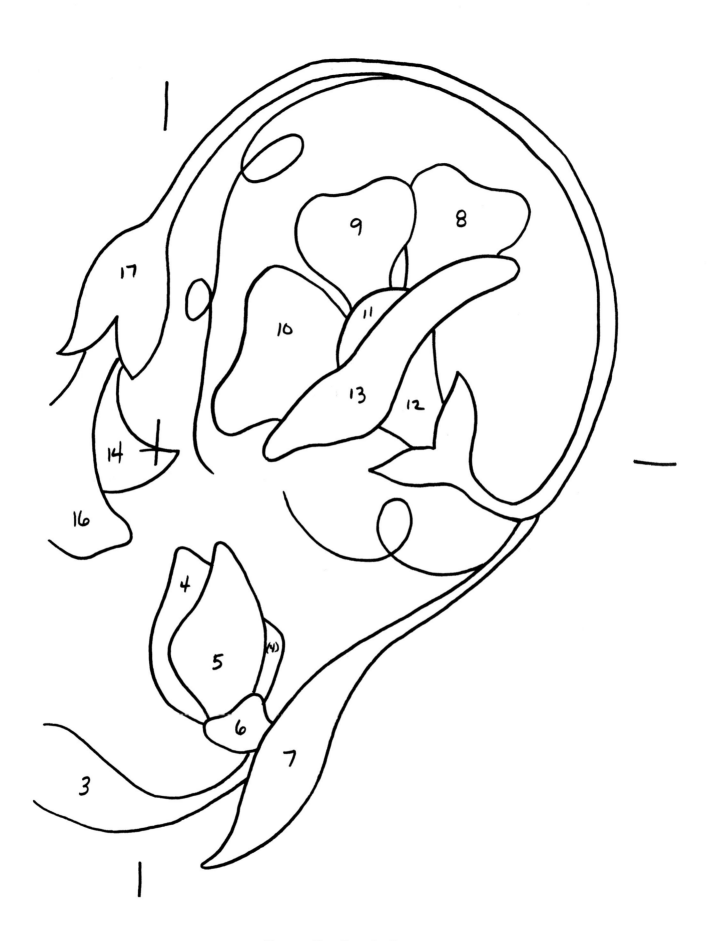

Hearts and Flowers

Don't let the narrowness of the stems scare you. Appliqué pieces #1 and #3 are easy to make. I used the 1/4" bias tape! Make the bias tape as you did in the Poppies block. Before stitching, trim away one of the turned–under edges of the bias tape by cutting along the fold (4-8). All you want to remove is the turned–under seam allowance, so don't cut too deeply. (It is important that when you made your bias tape that you fed the bias strip into the tool very evenly so that both turn–under edges are the same width.) Stitch the folded edge, as always, stitching the inside curve first. When you stitch the other side of the stem, use your needle to turn under the seam allowance taking care that your edge is smooth and your stitches don't show. You should have a stem half the width of the bias tape that you began with (4-9).

As you are piecing the flowers before appliquéing them to your background, don't forget to trim away the extra seam allowance that you left. Trim each seam allowance after stitching the seam and before adding the next piece. You will eliminate bulk and it will be much easier to quilt around each appliqué piece.

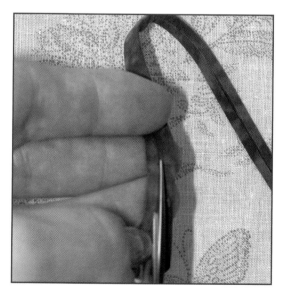

4-8

4-9

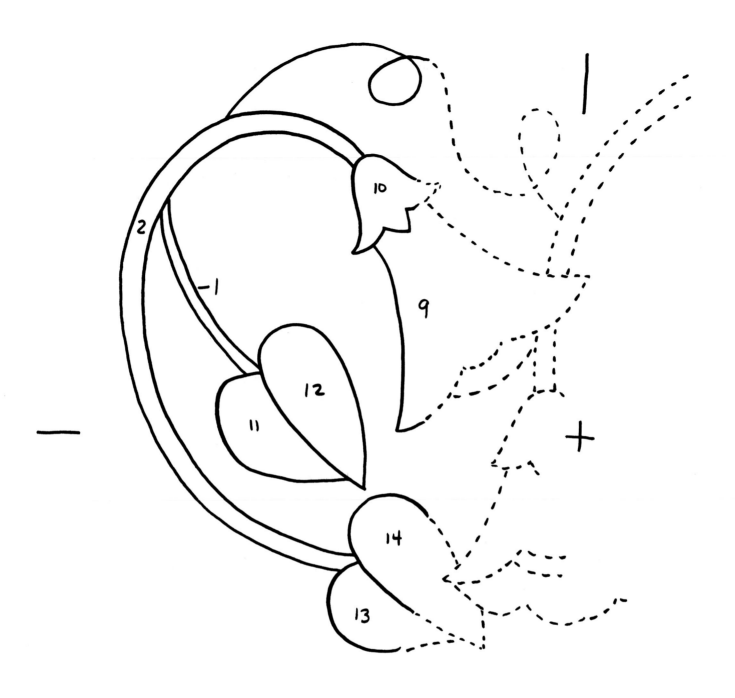

Hearts and Flowers

The Dahlia flower is pieced before appliquéing to the background. The heavy line on the pattern is the last seam you sew. When you trace the template onto your appliqué fabric and then cut your seam allowance, don't trim the seam allowance on the part of the petal that slides under the next petal. By leaving 1/2" or so you will have something on which you may pin the next appliqué piece. It is next to impossible to pin baste the next appliqué piece if you've only got a 3/16" overlap. In addition, it will be much easier for you to stitch. Remember, the seam allowance of the previous piece acts as "background" for the next piece.

Make sure that you begin stitching exactly where the petals come together in the center. After each seam is stitched, trim the seam allowance you left untrimmed. Be sure you trim the seam allowance before adding your next petal. Once you have added appliqué piece #28, slide #28 under #23 and appliqué that last seam. If you have been careful to begin at the exact center point on each petal, you will have a tightly fitting center and your flower unit will lay flat.

4-10

4-11

The dotted circle around the center represents a circle of French knots around the center. You may draw a line to follow with your knots or you can "eyeball" it. Use two strands of embroidery floss. Make a small quilter's knot on one end and clip the tail so that there won't be stray thread to shadow through to the front. Come up from behind the block onto the line. At the base of this thread, just next to the fabric, wrap the thread around the needle two or three times (*4-10*). Keeping the thread taught (don't let go of the thread), send your needle directly down into the block either through the same hole or very close to it (*4-11*). Pull the needle all the way through, holding that thread until the knot is formed snuggly next to the block. If you let go it will not be snug against the block. Bring your needle up again on the line and next to the knot (there is room for two French knots per petal) and repeat the process. After you have completed your last knot, travel the needle around and through the threads on the back (I don't make another knot) until the thread is anchored, keeping the threads as compact as possible. Then clip the excess.

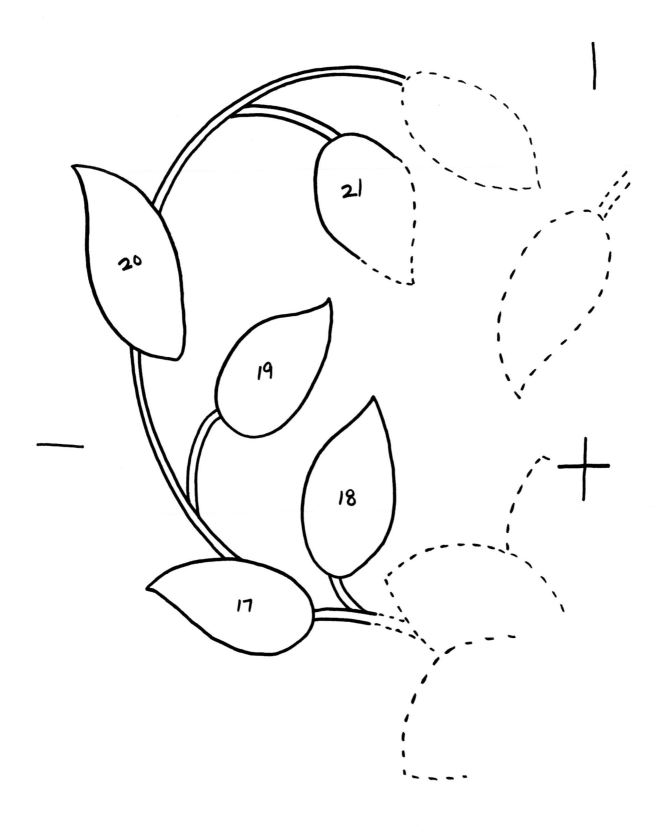

Hearts and Flowers

The stems for the bottom leaves can be made using the outline stitch that you used in the Fantasy block or a daisy stitch. The daisy stitch is a series of tiny loops.

Again, I wait until I have completed all of the appliqué before I include any embroidery. With a fine and light line, draw the stem lines onto your background and stretch your block in a 6" or 8" embroidery hoop. Again, it is up to you whether you use a single strand of embroidery floss or two. I like the delicate look of a single strand. Begin with the quilter's knot and bury it behind leaf # 14 (see Page 69). Bring your needle out from behind the leaf on the line you have lightly drawn on the background (the one to the right is actually the stem for #13). Put your needle back into the background in the same place it came out. Don't pull the thread all the way through, but, instead, leave a generous loop. Come back up to the top

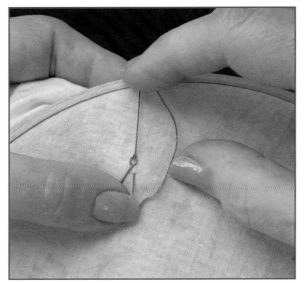

through the line that you have drawn on the background, just about 1/8th of an inch from where you began. As you bring the needle to the front of your block, pass it through the loop. When you pull the thread snug, you will have captured the loop. That's the daisy stitch. The next stitch, again, starts by passing the needle through the background at the same place you've just come to the top. Remember to leave a generous loop. Bring your needle up through the drawn line and the loop and pull the thread snug (4-12). Your last stitch needs securing or you will have a loop there with no reason. Just take your needle into the background on the other side of the loop from where the thread is coming from the back. When you pull the thread to the back, you will have secured the final loop. I thread the needle through the stitches, without catching the background fabric, for about an inch and clip the thread to secure.

4-12

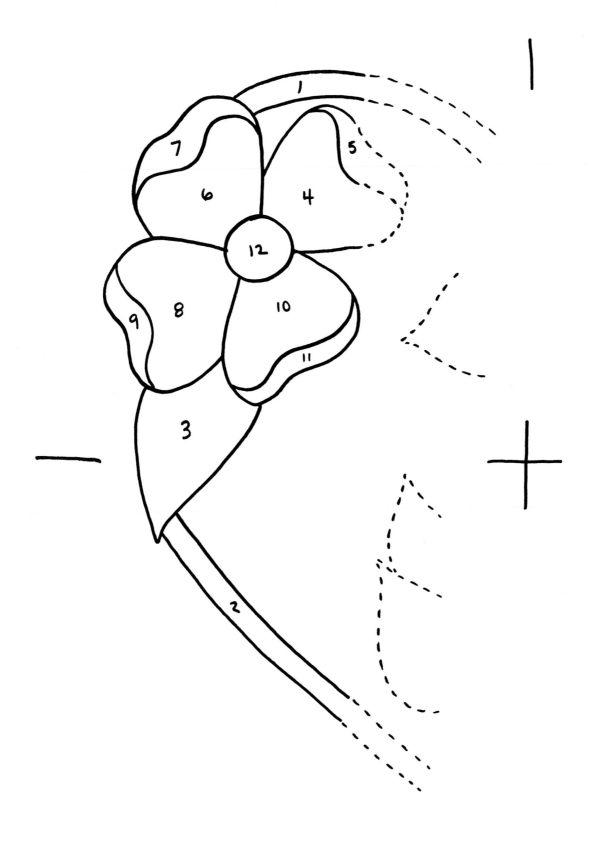

Hearts and Flowers

Hearts and Flowers

The flower buds, appliqué pieces #11-14, are each made of two pieces. Notice that both pieces have a sharp corner, made by a gracefully curved line intersecting another (much like a squashed "T"). It is easier to let the one fabric edge slide under the curve to create the sharp corner instead of having to stitch the point. But there are two "points" on the same seam so adjustments must be made. By snipping the seam allowance, one part can lay in one direction (sliding under the appliquéd edge) and the other part can lay in the other, giving you two sharp points without having to turn them.

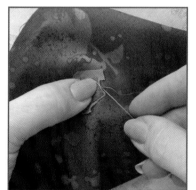

4-13

On the pattern there is a line that bisects the edge shared by the two appliqué pieces. There is an arrow on one piece and another on the other. The arrow represents the edge that is on top of the other. That's the part that you turn under with your needle. The part directly opposite the arrow is the part where the seam allowance slides under and is not turned.

4-14

When you trace the pattern, be sure to place the intersecting line and the arrows on the templates so you won't lose which is the top piece and which is the one that slips under.

Once you have trimmed your 3/16" seam allowance all the way around, clip it perpendicular to the template at the intersecting line on both appliqué pieces.

Slide the two pieces together in the clip with the sides indicated by the arrow on top (*4-13*). You will begin stitching from the center at the clip and work out, tie off, return to the center at the clip and work out in the other direction. If you are careful in turning under your seam allowances, including the turn–under line, you will have no stray threads peaking out from the "twist."

You may notice in this block that I have a thin appliqué "line" around the star-shaped center of the flowers. I appliquéd pieces #27 and #34 onto a lighter colored piece of fabric, leaving space between the two shapes. From about 1/16" from the turned–under edge of the star shape, I cut a 1/8" seam allowance. I appliquéd the combined piece to my block turning under the seam allowance just until a little of the lighter fabric peaked out (*4-14*). It almost looks as if I outlined the fabric with another fabric. This step is not that noticeable until you get right up to the quilt. But, then, I like to reward the person looking at my quilt with little surprises.

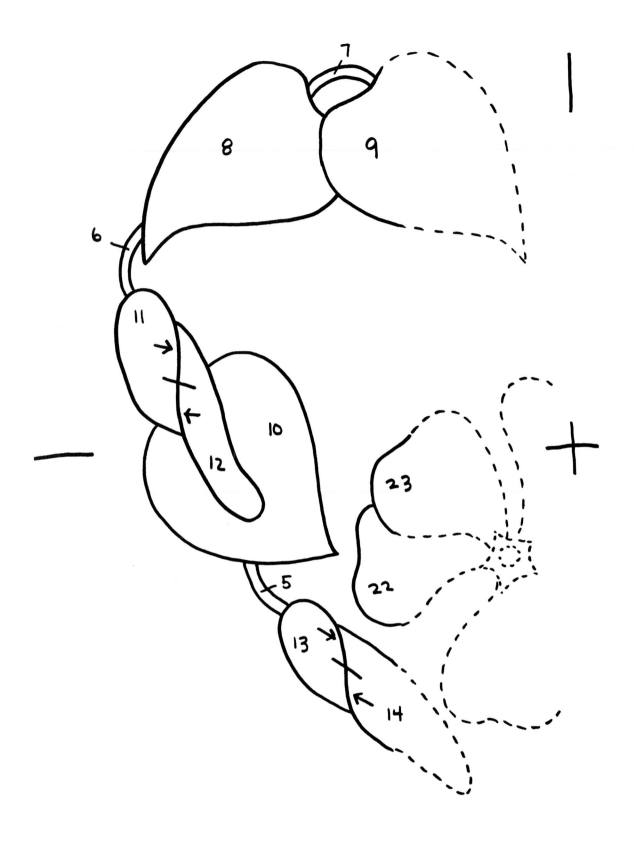

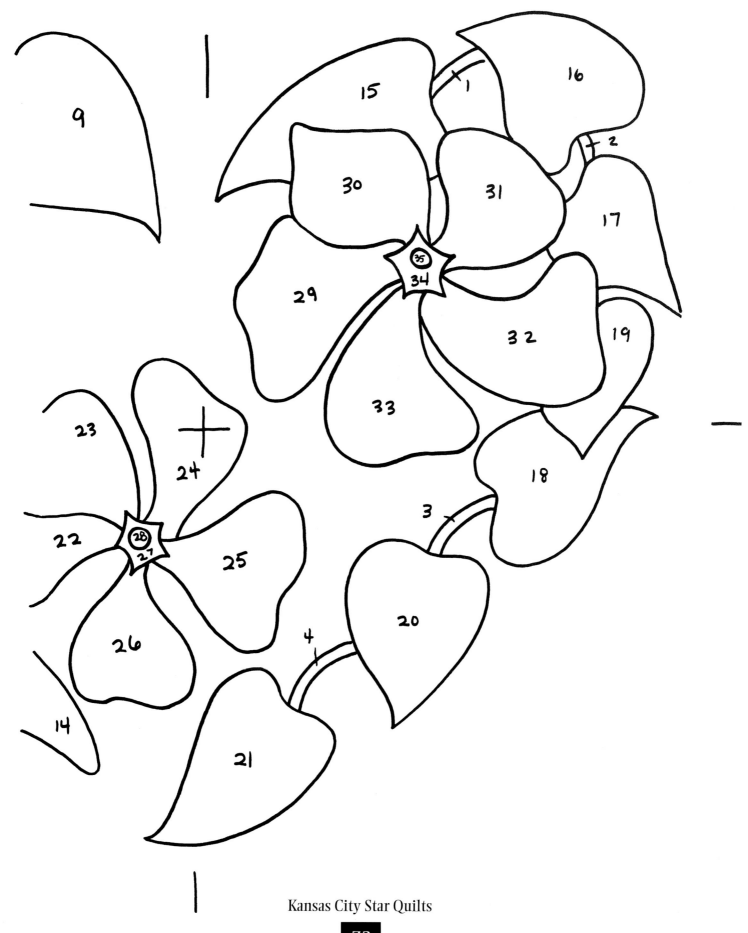

Hearts and Flowers

To create the basket, you might like to use one of two different techniques. To make my block I used my favorite tool for making bias tape. But you might like to try another technique, making bias tubes with Celtic Bias Bars. Your basket will have a little more dimension as the bias tubes have more layers of fabric involved.

Bias Bars are metal or plastic bars that come in a variety of widths from about 1/8" to 1/2". Begin by using your rotary cutter and ruler to cut bias strips. To determine the size, I double the width of the bar and add an inch. For instance, if the bar I'm using is 1/4" wide, I will make my strip about 1 1/2" wide. Remember using the string to measure and determine the length you'll need?

Fold the strip around the Bias Bar, wrong side together. Using the zipper foot on your sewing machine, sew the fabric next to the outside edge of the Bias Bar (you'll be trapping the bar inside). If your fabric is longer than the Bias Bar, sew almost to the end and slide the bar to the unsewn part. With the Bias Bar still inside the tube, trim the seam allowance so that it is no wider than half the width

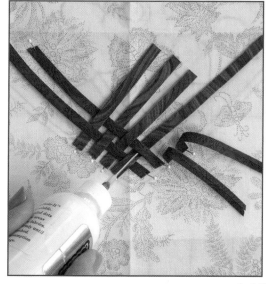

of the tube. Twist the seam so that it is centered, or just off center, over the flat side of the Bias Bar. Press the seam allowance to one side. Remove the tube. As you stitch the edges (be sure to stitch the inside curve first) you will be hiding the seam allowance underneath.

I placed my background block on the padded side of a combination rotary cutting mat and pressing mat. I used the overlay for placement and I just wove the bias tape to create the basket. The padded backing let me stick pins through the bias tape to hold it in place until I was ready to stitch. The dotted lines in the pattern indicate that I used one continous piece of bias tape (*4-15*).

Once you have all of the basket tapes in place, you may use a bit of glue to hold them in place at the intersections. I recommend a water-soluble glue designed for appliqué that comes in a small jar with a long thin tube to place the glue. It dries quickly and stays put unless you tug the pieces apart or you wash the block. (There are some appliqué artists who don't pin baste, they just place the appliqué pieces with tiny dollops of the glue.)

4-15

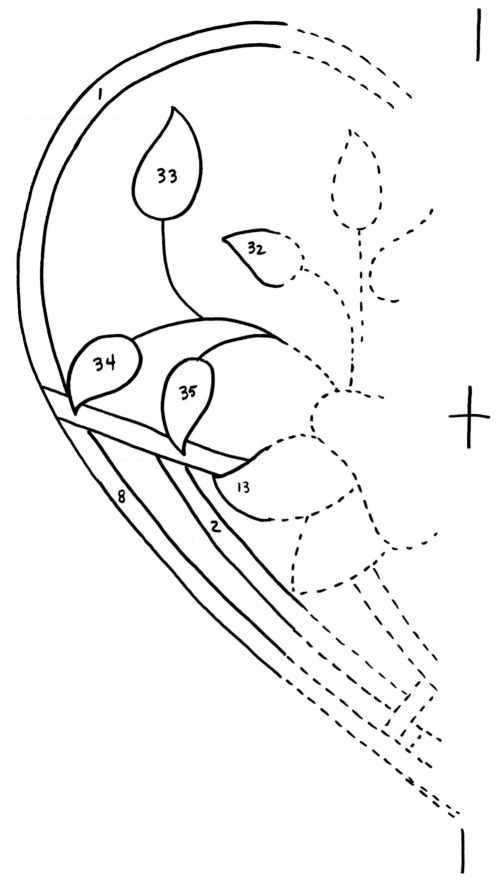

Hearts and Flowers

Hearts and Flowers

You'll notice that a lot of the techniques you have used in many of the blocks already completed are all used in this one block. The stems #2 and #7 are made with 1/4" bias tape. Because the bias tape is on the bias, it is easy to manipulate the fabric some to help you with the sharp curves of these two stems. Before placing and stitching the bias tape, stretch the outside edge. You can do this by pulling the folded edge that will serve as the outside edge. Just be careful that you don't also pull the edge that will serve as the inside edge. Stretch the entire outside edge by holding the bias tape between your index fingers and thumbs (right hand and left hand touching), pull to stretch, and then move to the next section (4-16). I'd say that you would be able to stretch no more than 1/4" at a time. If you want a tighter curve, repeat. Remember to stitch the inside curve first.

Stems #1, 11, 12 and #14 can be made with bias tape, too. Cut away one of the turned—under edges by cutting on the fold. Again, stitch the folded edge to the inside curve first and then use your needle to turn under the other edge. Stems #13 and #15 may be best accomplished using the cut away method. At least, that's how I did those stems. They were just too thin to cut out my seam allowance first.

The flowers are accomplished just as you did the Dahlia. The dark line is the last line you stitch. The little dots represent French knots. Notice that each petal again gets two knots placed slightly differently.

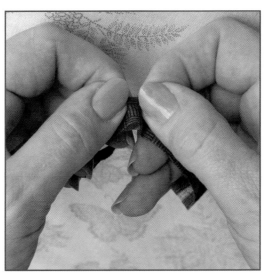

4-16

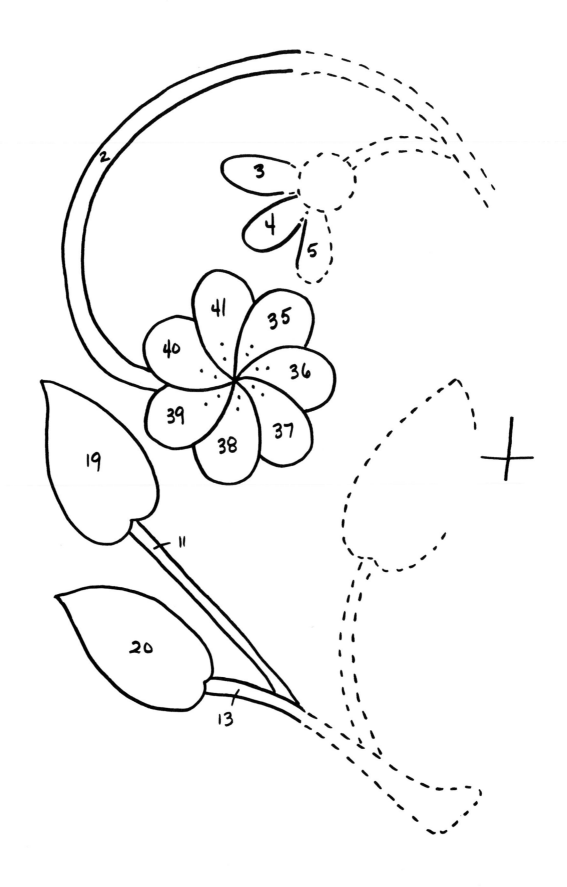

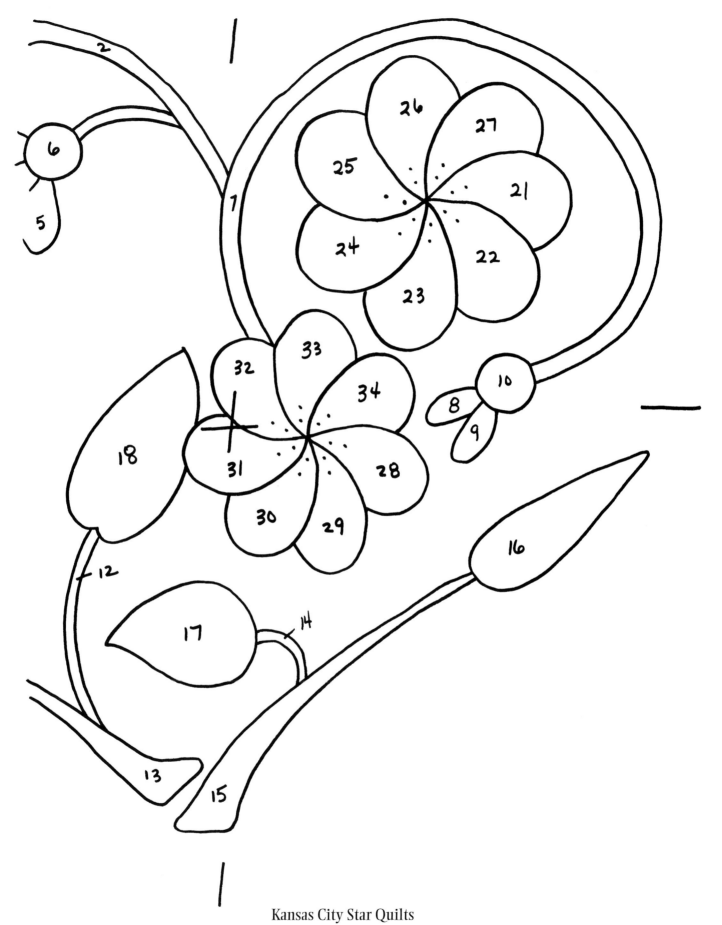

Hearts and Flowers

I wove the basket in this block the same way I did for the Rose Basket. I used the bias tape and I used continuous pieces. (Notice the dotted lines in the leaf, Page 84.)

I could have made bias tape for the stems, but appliqué piece #3 has such a sharp curve that I decided to use a freezer paper template instead. I felt that if I tried to use the bias tape, that inside curve would have had so much easing to fit that it would have puckered. I went ahead and used templates for all three stems since it was such a small amount. And because the pieces were relatively small and easy to handle, I cut my 1/8" seam allowance. I did pin baste in the left seam allowance, again, in the direction that I would be stitching, since the piece was so thin.

I pieced the leaves together before appliquéing them to the background. I also pieced the individual sunflowers before appliquéing them to the background (4-17). I really like the idea of being able to cut the background away from behind the appliqué to facilitate hand quilting. (See Page 99.) If you, too, decide to piece the flowers first,

be sure that you study the pattern carefully. Don't forget that you don't cut the narrow seam allowance where you need it to serve as the background to the piece you will stitch to it. And don't forget to trim that seam allowance before adding the next piece.

I know that the block looks complicated, especially if you piece the units first, but I think you'll find that it's not so bad. This is one of my favorite blocks.

4-17

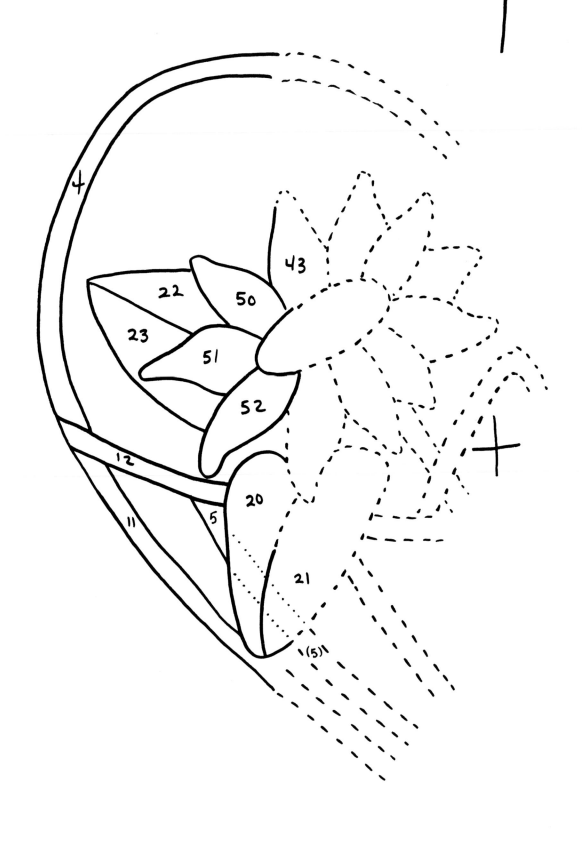

Hearts and Flowers

Hearts and Flowers

OK - here you are at your final examination! If you have made all the blocks in order, beginning with #1, you are ready and should have no trouble with this block! I have faith in you!

By now you are well aware that 1/8" stems are easily made with the bias tape-making tool. Trim away one of the turned–under edges, stitch the turned under edge to the inside curve first and then use your needle to turn–under the other side.

Don't let the flowers scare you. If you made the outline appliqué on the Vinca Vine Block, you can do this. It's the same thing only a little wider. Just remember to stitch in order of the stitching sequence. The lesser-numbered piece is appliquéd to a larger piece of fabric (I used yellow) and then the seam allowance is cut out around the appliquéd piece for the next numbered piece. In a few

places, you will be appliquéing the "yellow" fabric over the other. In this case, I recommend the cutaway method, sort of. By this I mean that I trimmed the seam allowance on the side where I began to stitch (remember Rule # 1!) but left enough fabric on the other side to pin baste (*4-18*).

Don't use a fabric with a really loose weave, such as homespun. Your seam allowances will fray too easily and you'll find it almost impossible to sew these thin, outlining, elements. I thought the dense weave of batik was good for the yellow fabric as I used only a 1/8" or less seam allowance in some places.

I pieced all of the flower units before appliquéing them to the background. I found it much easier to handle the flowers when I only had the small units to hold without the bulk of the background fabric as well.

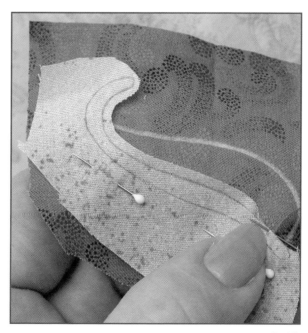

4-18

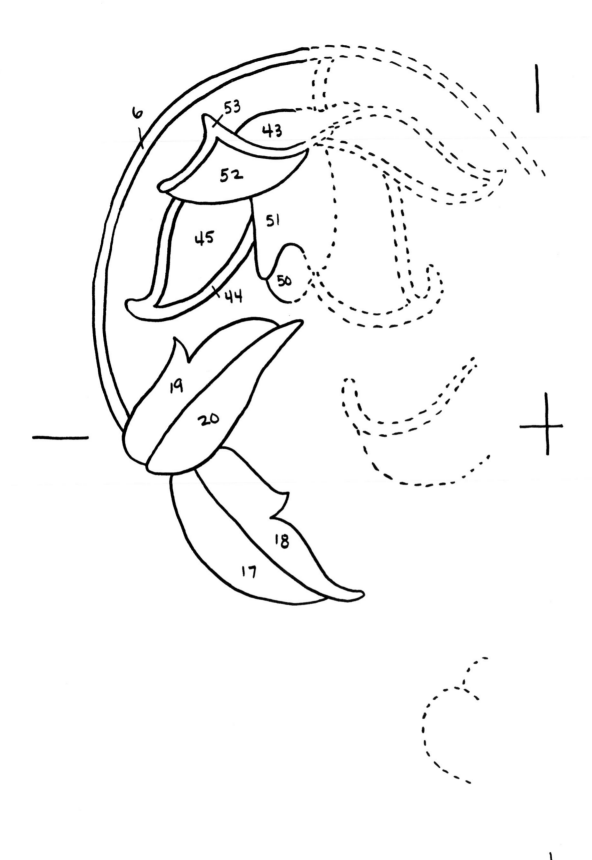

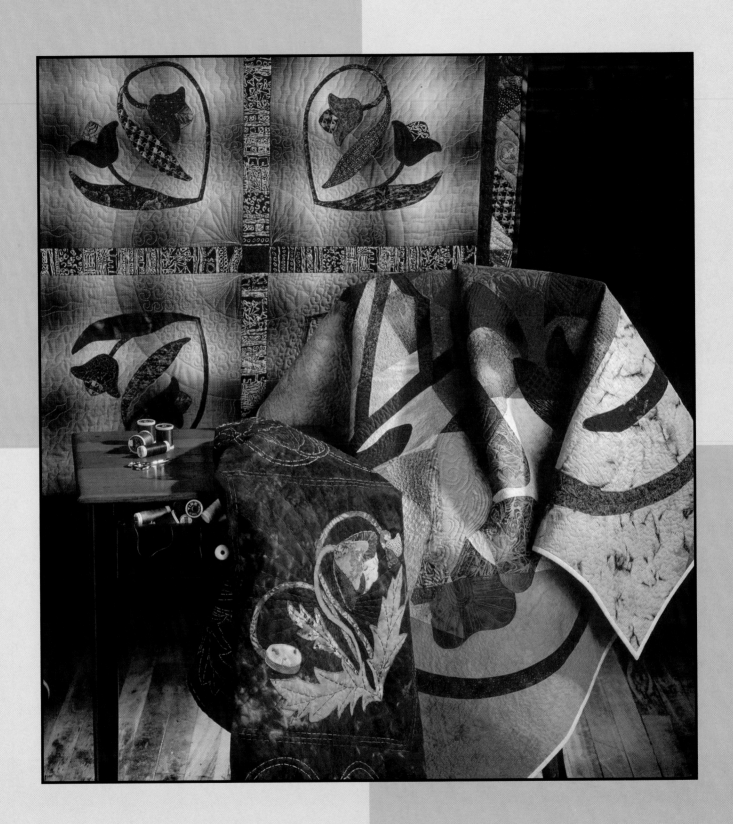

Hearts and Flowers

SQUARING THE BLOCKS

Once you have finished appliquéing the designs on all of your blocks, you are ready to square them up and prepare them for setting. The first step is to press the block, eliminating the wrinkles caused by handling the fabric while you were stitching.

With a clean fluffy terry towel over your ironing board, place the block, right side down. When you press, the appliqué will sink into the terry cloth and your dimension will not be lost. Remember, we are pressing the blocks, not ironing! That is, set the iron down onto the fabric and lift. Do not slide the iron back and forth. There is a big difference between the two motions! With your iron set on the steam setting, press the blocks until they are crisp and smooth. Steam can stretch your fabric, so be sure you press, not iron.

I like to use a 12 1/2" square rotary cutting ruler for 12" finished blocks. If my blocks are larger, I use the larger square rotary cutting ruler. In all likelihood, you will still be able to see your finger–pressed side-center and center markings. Center your rotary cutting ruler over these markings so that the 6 1/4" marking is through the center in both directions.

With your new or newly sharpened rotary cutting blade, cut the side and top edges of your block. Depen-ding on how much distortion you created in your appliqué work, and depending on the size of the background square with which you began, you may only be trimming 1/4" from either edge. Turn the block and line up the square ruler again. The newly cut raw edges will be at the edge of your 12 1/2" square ruler and the center and side-center markings will be at the 6 1/4" marks. Trim the other two sides. Repeat this process for all of the blocks and carefully set the blocks aside. If you have a favorite pizza store, you may be able to talk them out of a clean pizza box, large enough to hold your blocks without having to fold your blocks. You might take your 12 1/2" square rotary cutting ruler with you to the pizza store to show them what you need. OK, so if you have to buy the box, it will only be about 75 cents and is still worth the trouble of obtaining!

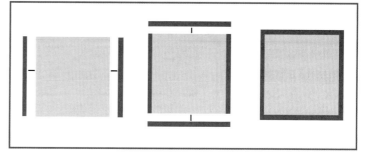

5-1

BORDER DESIGN

Hearts and Flowers

TEMPLATE A

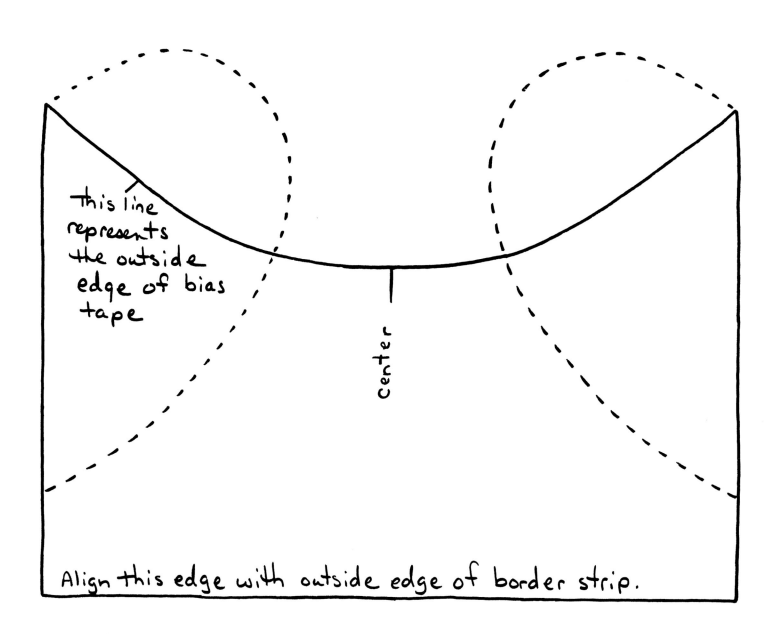

this line represents the outside edge of bias tape

Center

Align this edge with outside edge of border strip.

TEMPLATE B

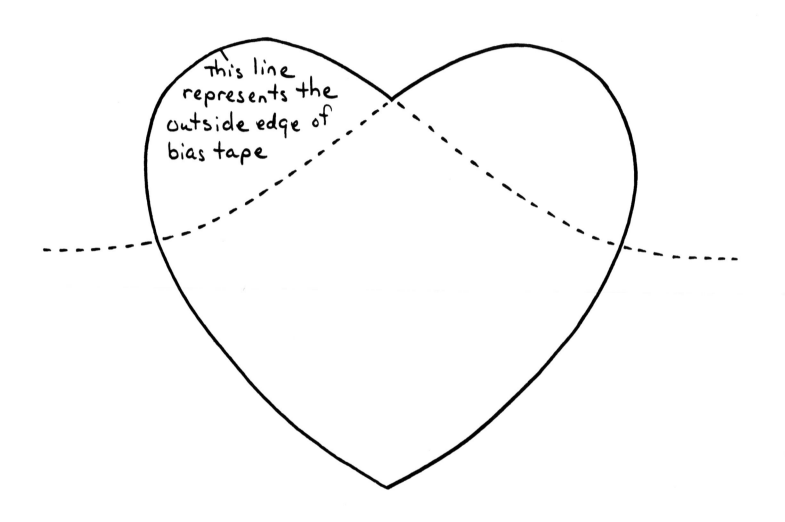

this line represents the outside edge of bias tape

Hearts and Flowers

under when you stitch the corners. At the far left, I stitched the left half of Template A but I left a really long tail so that I could connect to the corner hearts and it would appear seamless.

To mark the corner hearts with Template B, you are going to have to apply the borders and miter the corners first. So hold off until you get that far before worrying about the corners.

BIAS TAPE APPLIQUÉ

It appears as if the border design is one continuous bias tape with no breaks. Obviously this would be impossible to accomplish. Any breaks in the tape that I have made are hidden behind the overlapping tape. This way you can use some of your shorter lengths. However, I recommend that when you cut your bias strips for the tape, that you cut them as long as possible. This way you don't have to make as much tape and it is easier working with the longer lengths.

To cut the longest length of bias strip possible, you will have to fold your fabric from the bottom corner diagonally to the upper corner. If you have a really large piece, you may even have to make a second fold. Make the first fold by pulling the corner up to the opposite corner to make a large triangle.

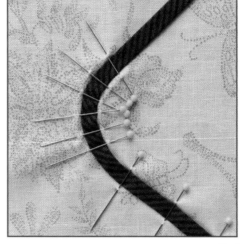

5-4

Smooth the fabric. Now, drag that same corner down (now two layers) in the same direction from which you started. Be sure to lift the corner edges and not the folded edge. You want to make sure that the fabric in the double fold (the second one you made) is snug and has created no gaps. Use the grid on your rotary cutting mat to make sure that both folded edges are exactly parallel to each other. If they are not, your cut bias strip will open out to look like a streak of lightning. Make some adjustments if you need to in order to keep those folds parallel, but be mindful that you don't open any gaps between the layers of fabric in the double fold.

With your rotary cutting ruler aligned so that it is exactly perpendicular to the folds, cut your bias strips (1/2" wide). Since I don't know how long your strips will be, I cannot tell you how many strips to cut. But I would start with 15 or 20. If you have to make more, there is no problem. I would suggest, though, that you try to leave the fabric undisturbed until you've finished your border or you will have to refold and straighten the cut edges.

When I pinned the border design in place, I did not use my appliqué pins. I was concerned about the slightest movement of the tape away from my line. I wanted my edge to be as smooth as possible. So I used longer pins.

I took a small bite into the background to the right of the tape, traveled over the bias tape and took a small bite into the background to the left of the tape. This held the bias tape in place without distorting it. I used lots of pins but only pinned enough bias tape to make one or two heart knots at a time. I removed the pins as I approached them in my stitching (5-4).

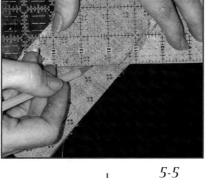

5-5

Once you have stitched the heart knot design to all four borders, you are ready to sew the borders to your quilt top.

MITERED CORNERS

5-6

Measure through the horizontal center of your quilt top to find out exactly how long the border should be. Find the exact center of the top border and measure out to each end half the measurement of the quilt top and mark the end with a pin. Find the exact center of the top of your quilt to which you will be applying the border. Pin the border to the quilt top, right sides together. Pin the border ends to the quilt top, aligning the pin with the

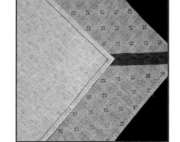

5-7

corner of the quilt top. Pin 1/4" in from the corner to mark where you will begin and end your stitching. Find the spot that is half way between the corner edge and the center pin and pin the border to the quilt top. This is how you center your border to the quilt top. With a 1/4" seam allowance, stitch the border to the quilt top, beginning 1/4" from the corner edge and ending 1/4" from the other corner edge. Press the seam allowance to the border.

Repeat the process with each of the three other borders.

I work this next step on my ironing board. To miter the corner, fold, with right sides together, the top right corner down to line up with the right edge of the quilt top. Align perfectly the seams that attach the borders. Place a few pins to keep this alignment secure. Make sure that the top border "tail" lies exactly over the right border. Again, place a few pins to maintain the alignment. Lay a long ruler exactly along the diagonal fold that you created and extend the ruler over the border strips. With a marker, make a line on the border that extends exactly from the fold to the outside edge of the border (5-5). This line should be 45 degrees from the outside edge of the border strips. Place a few pins over this line to secure against slippage when you move the quilt top to your sewing machine.

You will have to fold back the seam allowance between the border and the top so that you can begin stitching at the stitching line. Stitch from this point out to the outside edge, staying exactly on the line that you drew (5-6).

Back at the ironing board, open out the seam you just stitched and press the seam open. Trim the excess away so that you have remaining a 1/4" seam allowance. Press the inside corner of the miter flat (5-7).

Repeat the process at each of the other three corners.

THE CORNER APPLIQUÉ DESIGNS

5-8

Now that the corners are mitered, you can place the Template B and mark. Line up the center points of your heart exactly on the mitered seam. Notice that on my quilt I had to flatten out the "knot" tails a bit or the curve would have been too severe for smooth appliqué (5-8). The flattening of the tails will determine where you place Template B on the seam.

When you have finished appliquéing the border, you are ready to finish by quilting the quilt!

FINISHING

Cutting the background from behind the appliqué

Hand quilting is so much easier when you are only quilting through three layers; top, batting and backing. But appliqué is layering fabric on top of fabric. You may recall that I discussed piecing the appliqué units

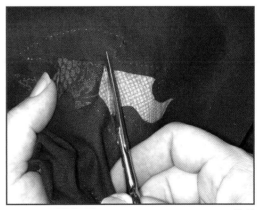

5-9

before stitching them to the background so that the background fabric behind the appliqué can be removed easily. That's where you regain that single layer.

I use my 4" knife-edge embroidery scissors. These are the sharp scissors with one blunt tip and one sharp tip. I begin by gently pinching the background fabric so as to separate it from the appliqué. With my scissors, I cut a tiny clip, just large enough to get the tip of my scissors into. With the blunt tip against the appliqué layer, I carefully clip the background fabric away from behind the appliqué, leaving a scant 1/4" seam allowance (5-9).

Now, remember that all of your appliqué is probably on the bias while the background is on the straight of grain. When you remove the background from behind the appliqué, you will notice that your block is a little more "stretchy" and has lost some of its strength. That is why I don't do any of this cutting until I am ready to sandwich the quilt top with the batting and backing.

By the way, if you plan to machine quilt your quilt, you don't need to cut the background fabric away from behind the appliqué.

THE QUILT SANDWICH

Measure your quilt top. Add 6" to this measurement in both directions and that is the size of the backing that I recommend. Begin by laying the fabric, wrong side up, on a table (if it is larger than the backing) or a clean floor. Using masking tape, tape the center of one side to your surface and then stretch the backing slightly and tape the opposite edge center. Stretching slightly, tape the center of another edge to the surface. Again, stretch slightly and tape the opposite edge center. Working from the center of an edge out to the corner and then the opposite edge, stretch and tape the backing to your table surface.

Carefully lay your batting over the backing, centering it. Your batting should be 4" wider and longer than your quilt top. Working from the center, and using your entire forearm and the flat of your hand, smooth the batting out to the edges. You don't really want to stretch the batting, but you do want to work out any ripples.

When the batting is smooth, lay the quilt top in the center of the batting. Again, use your whole hand and forearm to smooth, starting in the center and working out to the edges. If you are planning to hand quilt, you will want to thread baste the sandwich. If you are going to machine quilt, you can pin baste, using #1 safety pins, every 3". Either way, begin in the middle and work out to the edges. Here's an opportunity to find out just who your friends are. The job goes much faster if you can have company working with you! Remember, though, you have to be willing to work with them when they have quilts to baste!

When I thread baste, I like to use size 7 quilt basting needles. They are quite long and sturdy and make the job easier. I thread a bunch of the needles with a white thread (not my appliqué silks or fine cottons) that I cut a good 10 to 12 feet long, knotting one end. As I baste, I take stitches that are probably 1" long and 2" apart. I start in the middle and work out to the edge and turn and go the other direction. My basting lines are about 3" apart. I baste a grid in both directions and I baste a diagonal row of stitches from corner to corner in both directions (5-10). To tie off I simply make several stitches in place. When I have completely basted the whole top, I fold the backing over the exposed batting and baste the three layers together, protecting the edge of the batting while I quilt.

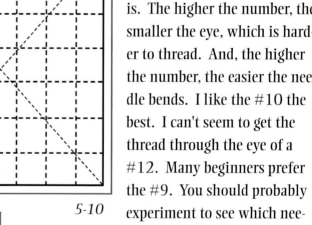

5-10

HAND QUILTING

I don't claim to be an expert quilter. So I don't want to tell you how to hand quilt. I recommend that you take classes or get a book that is devoted to hand quilting and written by someone who is an expert. But I will tell you some things that I have found to be helpful.

Hand quilting is done with a very short needle, called a between. The shorter the needle, the more control you have. The higher the size number, the thinner the shaft is. The higher the number, the smaller the eye, which is harder to thread. And, the higher the number, the easier the needle bends. I like the #10 the best. I can't seem to get the thread through the eye of a #12. Many beginners prefer the #9. You should probably experiment to see which needle you like the best.

Most people wear their thimble on the middle finger of their dominant hand. I actually use my index finger instead. I have much more dexterity and control with my index finger than my middle finger. The needle is not actually held between your fingers when you quilt but is balanced against the thimble.

I don't use anything to protect my finger under the quilt. I have learned that if I am pricking my finger, causing pain, I am taking too big of a stitch. If I can keep from pricking my finger deep enough to hurt, my stitches are pretty small.

I recommend that you quilt around all of your appliqué pieces. This really adds dimension to your quilt. What you do in the space considered background is up to you and you have lots of choices. One of the most classic looks behind appliqué is diagonal cross-hatching. It may be perpendicular so as to create an over-all pattern of squares. A "hanging diamond" design is a series of lines at a 60-degree angle. You can vary the width of the space between your diagonal lines or be very consistent. Experiment with the look you like best. But a contrast between the soft curves of your appliqué and the sharp angles created by the cross-hatching is very appealing to the eye.

5-11

5-12

BINDING ACCENT

Once the quilting is done and before the binding is added, there is a special touch that I like to add to my quilts that give them a distinctive look. I call it a binding accent because it is just next to the binding. Some quilters slip in a folded strip of fabric as they sew the binding. This is a flange and is an added element that can cover some of the design. My accent becomes part of the design and actually acts as another border, even though it is only 1/8" wide. It actually looks like a flat "piping."

From the binding accent fabric, you have cut (7) 7/8" strips. Cut one of the strips into (2) 7/8" x 22" strips. With a diagonal seam, sew two 44" strips together, repeating so that you end up with two strips about 88" long. Sew the half-strips to each of two strips so that you end up with (2) strips about 66" long.

I use my walking foot to apply the accent strips to my quilt top. I apply the side strips first (for absolutely no reason but that the framing strips are added to the blocks in that order). Line up the strip with the raw edge of the quilt top and right side to the quilt top. Use the side of the walking foot as your guide along the edge. It is imperative that you maintain a constant distance from the edge, or your accent will not be even. The needle should be in the middle position or about 1/8" to the left of the far right position (5-11).

Very carefully, sew the strip to the edge of the quilt top. If you find yourself wavering in your stitch line, back up and fix it. It is important that the raw edges exactly align as well.

In the same way, sew a strip to the opposite side. When you begin to add the top and bottom strips, fold the sewn strip back toward the raw edge as you sew the other strip over it so it is finished in the corner. When all the strips have been sewn in place, fold and finger press the seam (*5-12*). Now you are ready to add the binding. The process is the same if you've added the accent or not.

5-13

BINDING

Once the quilting is all completed, you can remove the basting threads. At this point you are ready to add the final touch that holds the whole thing together and finishes the edges. This is the binding. There are many ways to accomplish the binding and there are many good books that describe various finishing edges. I'm just going to tell you how I do my binding.

5-14

To begin with, I measure around the

circumference of the quilt and divide this number by 40, the average usable amount of fabric most often found in a fabric, cut selvage to selvage. This will give me the number of strips that I will need to cut from my binding fabric. If the number is a fraction (i.e. 6.725 as in the case of my quilt) I round up to the next whole number. I usually cut my strips 2 1/2" wide. (I multiply the number of strips by 2 1/2" and that gives me the least amount of binding fabric I need to buy. I round that number up so I can have enough room to straighten the fabric and cut a strip incorrectly without running out.)

When I've cut the correct number of strips (in the example above I would cut 7), I sew them all together, end-to-end, with a diagonal seam. I press the seams open and trim the seam allowance to 1/4". I fold the strip in half, length-wise, with wrong sides together, and press the fold the entire length of the binding strip.

Leaving a tail of about 10", I line up the double raw edge of the binding strip to the outer edge of my quilt top, starting somewhere to the right of the middle of the top edge of my quilt. At this point I have not trimmed away any of the excess batting and backing. I don't do that until I have attached the binding.

I use a walking foot on my sewing machine. This feeds the top layer and the bottom layer evenly as I sew. I use the right side of the walking foot as a guide against the raw edges of the binding and quilt. I move the needle to the far right position. I would say that my seam allowance is slightly larger than a 1/4". I lengthen my stitches slightly since I have more thickness than when I piece.

At the corner, I stop stitching slightly more than 1/4" from the edge. In other words, the stitching ends the same distance from the end as the stitching is from the edge. I pull the quilt from the machine to loosen the grip at the corner, but I don't cut my threads. I turn the quilt so that I have turned the corner. I pull the binding strip up at a 45-degree angle

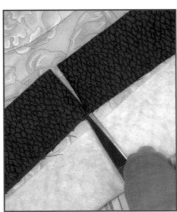

from the stitching. This makes a diagonal fold from the stitching to the corner of the quilt top (5-13). The raw edge of the binding and the

5-15

raw edge of the quilt top are in a straight line. If they aren't, it is probably because I stitched beyond where I should have. If that's the case, I clip the last stitch to be able to pull the binding back further.

I fold the binding straight down so that the raw edge is once again aligned with the edge of the quilt top and the second fold is parallel to the top edge (5-14). Beginning a few stitches into the excess batting, I begin stitching the binding to the second side of the quilt top.

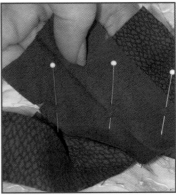

At the next corner I repeat the mitering described above.

When I have gone all the way

5-16

around the quilt and am approaching the starting place with the free tail, I stop stitching about 12" to 15" away from where I began. To connect the tails so that I have a smooth join, I bring the binding tails together in the middle of the open space. I fold the tails back on themselves so that there is a 1/8" gap where the tails meet at the folds. Keeping the folds intact, I bridge the 1/8" gap so that the folds meet. I make a small perpendicular clip through all four layers where the folds meet (5-15).

With the back of the quilt facing me, I open the binding strips out and lay the two strips across each other, right sides together (right tail over the left). The clips on the right tail line up with the top edge of the left tail and the clips on the left tail line up with the left edge of the right tail (5-16). I pin the two strips together and stitch from the upper left corner to the lower right corner of where the tails cross at a 45-degree angle (5-17).

I press the seam open and trim the seam allowance to 1/4". I fold the strip again at the join, wrong sides together and press the crease. I sew the joined binding strip to the edge of the quilt between where I ended stitching and began stitching.

Once the binding is attached, I cut away the excess batting and backing. When I cut I let just a peak of the batting stick out farther than the edge of the binding. I want to be sure that the batting fills my binding and that there is no empty space between the folds of the binding.

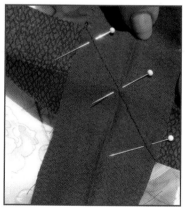

Now I'm ready to sew the folded edge to the back of the quilt. I use

5-17

the same stitch I do when I appliqué so my stitches are hidden.

I use the same color thread as the binding. I cover the machine stitching with the fold of the binding. At the corners I tuck the fold that is created by the mitered corner in the opposite direction that the front fold is facing. This distributes the bulk (5-18).

When you have completely sewn the binding to the quilt you are ready to make a label documenting the quilt; include your name, address, designer, who you made the quilt for and why, the date completed and any other information you'd like your descendants to know about your quilt. I have included a pattern for a label that you can either appliqué or draw with permanent marking pens. Attach the label to the bottom right corner of the back of the quilt.

5-18

Congratulations on completing your quilt! I hope that you enjoy the gallery and are inspired to use these patterns in a variety of ways!

LABEL PATTERN

Hearts and Flowers

"Kathy's Hobby," 47" x 47"
by Kathryn Berner, Prairie Village, Kan., 2002.
Machine quilted by Dana Davis.

Hearts and Flowers

"Hearts and Flowers in Pastel Pinkwork," 51" x 51"
by Pat Moore and Carol Kirchhoff, 2002.
Hand quilted by Helen Bergsieker.

"Bluebell Pillow," 15" x 15"
by Nancy Nunn, Bonner Springs, Kan., 2002.

Hearts and Flowers

"Hearts and Flowers,"
22 1/2" x 58"
by Linda Mooney,
Shawnee, Kan., 2002.

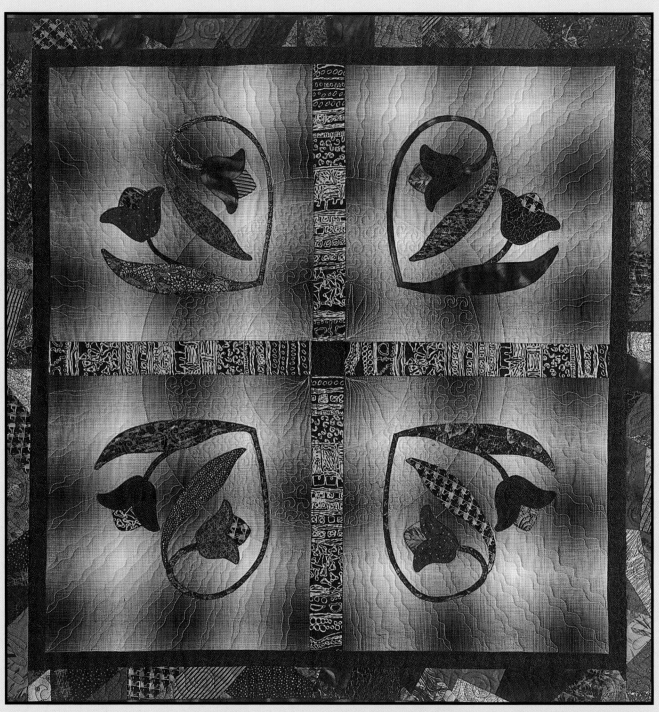

"Sunshine and Flowers," 38 3/4" x 38 3/4"
by Charlotte Gurwell, Overland Park, Kan., 2002.

Sweater, Vinca Vine, by Judy Oberkrom, Leawood, Kan., 2002.
Trapunto pillow by Kathy Delaney, Overland Park, Kan., 2002.

"Fantasy," 56 1/2" x 46"
by Leanne M. Baraban, Overland Park, Kan., 2002.

"The Splendid Poppy," 35" x 35"
by Linda Potter, Overland Park, Kan., 2002.

"Two silk jumpers,"
by Jeanne Poore, Overland Park, Kan., 2002.

Hearts and Flowers

INDEX OF PATTERNS

Here is a chronological list — including repeats — of the quilt patterns and designs published by The Kansas City Star from 1928 to the present.

If you'd like to see the patterns on the pages of the newspaper, microfilm copies of The Star are available at the Kansas City Public Library's Main Branch, 311 E. 12th St., Kansas City, Mo.

Patterns since 2001 are available in books only. Call 816-234-4636 for information.

Months not listed here had no published quilt patterns.

1928
- September
  Pine Tree
  Album Quilt
- October
  French Star
  Log Cabin
  Rob Peter and Pay Paul
  Cherry Basket
  Wedding Ring
- November
  Jacob's Ladder
  Greek Cross
  Sky Rocket
  Double T
- December
  Ocean Wave
  Wild Goose Chase
  Old Maid's Puzzle
  Rambler

1929
- January
  Weathervane
  Monkey Wrench
  Spider Web
  Irish Chain
- February
  Rising Sun
  Princess Feather
  Double Nine Patch
  Eight-Pointed Star
- March
  Goose in the Pond
  Dove in the Window
  Beautiful Star
  Broken Circle
  Beggar Block
- April
  Cupid's Arrow Point
  Noon Day Lily
  Lafayette Orange Peel
  Necktie
- May
  Duck and Ducklings
  House on the Hill
  Crossed Canoes
  Turkey Tracks

- June
  Ribbon Border Block
  Posey
  Bird's Nest
  Crosses and Losses
  Double Star
- July
  Jack in the Box
  Aircraft
  Springtime Blossoms
  Sunbeam
- August
  Saw-Tooth
  Cross and Crown
  Hands All 'Round
  Honey Bee
  Flower Pot
- September
  Susannah
  Goose Tracks
  Fish Block
  Wedding Ring
- October
  Swastika
  Seth Thomas Rose
  "V" Block
  Little Beech Tree
- November
  Palm Leaf
  Tulip Applique
  Mill Wheel
  Order No. 11
  Old King Cole's Crown
- December
  Strawberry Block
  Old King Cole
  Little Wooden Soldier
  Road to Oklahoma
  (The "Santa's Parade Quilt" series ran in December 1929).

1930
- January
  Churn Dash
  Corn and Beans
  Rose Cross
  Milky Way
- February
  True Lovers Buggy Wheel

  Indiana Puzzle
  Blazing Star
  Aster
- March
  Sunflower
  Grape Basket
  Steps to the Altar
  Kaleidoscope
  Dutchman's Puzzle
- April
  English Flower Garden
  Single Wedding Ring
  Pin Wheels
  Cross and Crown
- May
  Missouri Puzzle
  Merry Go-Round
  Lone Star
  Missouri Star
  Sail Boat
- June
  Virginia Star
  Rail Fence
- July
  Mexican Star
  Basket of Oranges
  Rose Album
  Clay's Choice
- August
  Maple Leaf
  Sunbonnet Sue
  Compass
  Kaleidoscope
  Rainbow Tile
- September
  Goblet
  Calico Puzzle
  Broken Dishes
  Swallows in the Window
- October
  Secret Drawer
  Spider Web
  Marble Floor
  Pinwheel
  (The "Memory Bouquet Quilt" series ran in October 1930.)
- November
  Grandmother's Favorite
  Indian Emblem

  Friendship
  Puss in the Corner
  Sage-Bud
  (The "Memory Bouquet Quilt" series ran in November 1930).
- December
  Turnabout "T"
  Snow Crystals
  Sweet Gum Leaf
  Rose Dream

1931
- January
  Silver and Gold
  Tennessee Star
  Flower Pot
  Greek Cross
  Sheep Fold
- February
  Amethyst
  Wheel of Mystery
  Pontiac Star
  Baby Bunting
- March
  Seven Stars
  Rebecca's Fan
  French Bouquet
  Casement Window
- April
  Basket of Lilies
  King's Crown
  June Butterfly
  Fence Row
- May
  Indian Trail
  English Ivy
  Jackson Star
  Dutch Tulip
  Love Ring
- June
  Ararat
  Iris Leaf
  Ozark Diamond
  Kite Quilt
- July
  Cactus Flower
  Arrowhead Star
  Giddap
  Sugar Loaf

INDEX OF PATTERNS

- August
  Cross Roads
  Bachelor's Puzzle
  Morning Star
  Pineapple Quilt
  Dresden Plate
- September
  Stepping Stones
  Tennessee Star
  Chips and Whetstones
  Boutonniere
- October
  Prickly Pear
  Castle Wall
  Butterfly
  Pickle Dish
  Dutch Tile
- November
  Cottage Tulips
  Formosa Tea Leaf
  Bridge
  Evening Star
- December
  Poinsettia
  Goldfish
  Christmas Star
  Crazy Daisy

1932
- January
  Friendship Knot
  Circular Saw
  Heart's Desire
  Job's Tears
  Necktie
  (The "Horn of Plenty Quilt"
  series also ran in January 1932).
- February
  Autograph Quilt
  Hour-Glass
  Spring Beauty
  Grandmother's Basket
  (The "Horn of Plenty Quilt"
  series also ran in February 1932).
- March
  Grandmother's Favorite
  Quilting Design
  Shamrock
  Magnolia Bud
- April
  Nose-Gay
  Diamond Field
  Red Cross
  Solomon's Puzzle
  "4-H" Club
- May
  Russian Sunflower
  Storm at Sea

Crow's Nest
Garden Maze
- June
  Cowboy's Star
  Ducklings
  Lend and Borrow
  Wheel of Fortune
- July
  Flying Bats
  Log Cabin
  Gretchen
  Double Nine Patch
  Kansas Star
- August
  Liberty Star
  Golden Glow
  Square Deal
  Purple Cross
- September
  Farmer's Wife
  Interlocked Squares
  Dove in the Window
  Florida Star
- October
  Interlocked Squares
  Pineapple Cactus
  Crazy Anne
  Old Missouri
  Clam Shells
  (A diagram of the "Happy Childhood Quilt"
  ran in October 1932.
- November
  Puss in the Corner
  Christmas Tree
  Christmas Toy Quilt
  Four Winds
  (The "Happy Childhood Quilt"
  also ran in October 1932.
- December
  Corner Posts
  Snow Crystal
  Pilot's Wheel
  Christmas Tree
  Star of Hope

1933
- January
  Star of Hope
  Old Spanish Tile
  Arkansas Star
  Star-shaped Quilting Design
  Floral Pattern Quilting Design
- February
  Sunflower Motif Quilting Design
  Petal and Leaf Quilting Design
  Medallion Quilting Design
  Pilot's Wheel
- March

Arkansas Star
Lone Star of Paradise
Bouquet in a Fan
Nest and Fledgling
- April
  St. Gregory's Cross
  Guiding Star
  Light and Shadow
  Flowing Ribbon
  Friendship Star
- May
  Broken Crown
  Square Within Square
  Oklahoma Sunburst
  Points and Petals
- June
  Square and Points
  Little Giant
  Puss in the Corner
  Double Arrow
- July
  Bridal Stairway
  Air-Ship Propeller
  Bridge Quilt
  Indian Canoes
  Flying Swallows
- August
  Double Pyramid
  Economy
  Triplet
  Jack in the Pulpit
- September
  Broken Stone
  Cypress
  Cheyenne
  Glory Block
- October
  Square and Half Square
- November
  Poinsettia
  Ozark Trail
  Four Crown
  Crow's Nest
- December
  Circle Upon Circle
  Arkansas
  Christmas Tree
  Morning Glory
  Charm Quilt

1934
- January
  Star Center on French Bouquet
  Double Irish Chain
  London Stairs
  Franklin D. Roosevelt
- February
  New Album

Valentine Quilt
Dogwood Blossom
Cat's Cradle
- March
  Kansas Trouble
  Water Glass
  Eight Pointed Star
  Broken Circle
  Little Boy's Breeches
- April
  Pin-Wheel
  Jinx Star
  Oklahoma Sunburst
  Texas Pointer
- May
  Snowball Quilt
  Windmill Star
  Flowering Nine-Patch
  Joseph's Coat
- June
  Christmas Tree
  Lover's Lane
  Crystal Star
  Wagon Wheels
  Friendship Quilt
- July
  Triple Star
  Gordian Knot
  Red Cross
  Airplane
- August
  Japanese Garden
  Feather Edge Star
  Saw Tooth
  Sunflower Design Pattern
- September
  Dogwood Design Pattern
  Border and Block Design Pattern
  Lotus Leaf Design Pattern
  Whirling Pin Wheel
  New Album
- October
  Hazel Valley Cross Roads
  Jacob's Ladder
  Arrow Star
  Friendship Quilt
- November
  Quilting Motif Design Pattern
  Square Design Pattern
  Floral Motif Design Pattern
  Quilts and Gifts Design Pattern
- December
  Marble Quilt
  Cluster of Lillies

1935
- January
  Arabic Lattice

INDEX OF PATTERNS

Coffee Cups
Fan Quilt
- February
Old-Fashioned String Quilt
Arkansas Snowflake
Friday the 13th
Wedding Ring
- March
Missouri Daisy
Bridle Path
Farmer's Daughter
Arabic Lattice
- April
My Graduation Class Ring
Goldfish
Ozark Trail
Tulip Quilt
- May
Grandmother's Basket
Churn Dash
Twinkle, Twinkle Little Star
Indian Hatchet
Old Missouri
- June
String Quilt
Strawberry
Florida Star
Twinkle, Twinkle Little Star
- July
Jacob's Ladder
Sonnie's Play House
Shaded Trail
Grandma's Brooch
Flower Basket
- August
Wind Mill
Diamond Circle
Railroad Crossing
Leaves and Flowers
Teapot
- September
Gold Bloom
Hands All Around
Apple Leaf
Four Leaf Clover
- October
Melon Patch
Arkansas Meadow Rose
Scrap Bag
Pine Cone
Album
- November
Squirrel in a Cage
Cog Wheels
Snail Trail
Compass and Chain
Broken Branch
- December

Basket of Flowers
Ozark Star
Shaded Trail
Kansas Dust Storm

1936
- January
Missouri Wonder
Flower of Spring
Circle Saw
Arrow Head
- February
Morning Star
White Lily
Seven Stars
Kansas Beauty
Young Man's Invention
- March
Wood Lily or Indian Head
Star Sapphire
Pointing Star
IXL or I Excel
- April
Butterfly
Dove at the Window
Quilter's Pride
Martha Washington
- May
Dog Quilt
Patriotic Star
Ma Perkin's Flower Garden
Cups and Saucers
Sickle
- June
Dove at the Window
Turkey Tracks
Jupiter Star
Lover's Link
- July
Hidden Star
Airport
Marble Quilt
- August
Anna's Pride
Star
- September
Whirligig Hexagon
Landon Sunflower
Chinese Puzzle
Rising Sun
- October
Ozark Cobblestone
Peggy Anne's Special
Happy Hunting Grounds
Mayflower
Dragonfly
- November
Basket of Diamonds

Mountain Road
Solomon's Temple
Rolling Stone
- December
Circle and Square
Grandmother's Tulip
Modern Broken Dish

1937
- January
The Kite
Arkansas Centennial
Flower Pot
Square Diamond
Whirling Star
- February
Nosegays
Four-Pointed Star
Golden Circle Star
- March
Right Hand of Fellowship
Waves of the Sea
Spool Quilt
Old-Fashioned Goblet
Double "T"
- April
Quilt Without a Name
Dolly Madison
Ozark Tile
Star of Bethlehem
- May
Owl Quilt
Flower Garden Block
Depression
Diamond Cross
Winding Blade
Maple Leaf
- June
Album Quilt
Old Maid's Puzzle
Midget Necktie
- July
Flying Kite
Double Square
Indian Star
Russian Sunflower
- August
Ozark Sunflower
Hanging Basket
Basket of Diamonds
Broken Dish
- September
Verna Belle's Favorite
Broken Window
Old-Fashioned Quilt
Bear's Paw
Arrowhead
Necktie

- October
Modern Broken Dish
Clay's Choice
Winged Square
Quilting Design for Many Quilts
Lotus Quilting Design
- November
Modified Floral Quilting Design
Circular Quilting Design
Tulip Motif Quilting Design
Conventional Quilting Design
Favorite Quilting Design
- December
Motif Quilting Design
Household Quilting Design

1938
- January
Quilt of Variety
Ladies' Aid Album
Old-Fashioned Wheel
- February
Electric Fan
- March
Border Quilting Design
Fair and Square
Texas Flower
- April
Twentieth Century Star
Broken Square
Letha's Electric Fan
- May
Jig Jog Puzzle
Bethlehem Star
Basket
Rebecca's Fan
North Star
Friendship Quilt
- June
Pin Wheel
Blockade
- July
Chinese Block
Little Boy's Breeches
Heart of the Home
- August
Versatile Quilting Design
Friendship Quilt
Maple Leaf
- September
Double Cross
Friendship Quilt
- October
Six-Pointed Star
Flying "X"
- November
Contrary Husband
Floating Clouds

Kansas City Star Quilts

INDEX OF PATTERNS

Right Hand of Fellowship
White Square
- December
Wild Goose

1939
- January
Sandhills Star
- February
"T" Quilt
Small Wedding Ring
- March
Windmill
Wandering Flower
Pig Pen
- April
Farmer's Field
Sun Rays
- May
Swastika
Thrifty Wife
Crazy Tile
Chisholm Trail
- June
Lost Golsin'
Hexagon Beauty
Oak Grove Star
Pride of Ohio
- July
"X" Quartette
Double "T"
Rolling Stone
- August
Pine Burr
Corner Star
Broken Star
- September
Little Boy's Britches
Rosebud
Star and Box
Red Cross
- October
Our Country
Lost Paradise
Broken Path
- November
Crown of Thorns
Flag In, Flag Out
Buckeye Beauty
- December
Rosalia Flower Garden
Sylvia's Bow
Thrifty

1940
- January
Air Plane
Bluebell

Ladies' Fancy
- February
4-H
Six Point String
Little Cedar Tree
- March
Hicks Basket
Fan and Ring
- April
Silent Star
Cabin Windows
- May
Mother's Favorite Star
Comfort Quilt
Around the World
Flower Ring
- June
Mona's Choice
Long 9 Patch
Garden Walk
- July
The "X"
Double "V"
Whirl Around
- August
E-Z Quilt
Jig Saw Puzzle
Quilter's Fan
- September
Car Wheel
Winged Nine Patch
Spider Web
- October
Hexagon Star
Garden Patch
- November
Southside Star
- December
Carrie Nation
Spool Quilt
Springtime in the Ozarks
Four Patch Fox and Goose

1941
- January
Colorado Quilt
Red Cross
- February
Mother's Choice
Cotton Boll
Anna's Choice
- March
Four Red Hearts
Arkansas Cross Roads
- April
Seven Sisters
Whirling Star
Mosaic

- May
Missouri Sunflower
Fence Row
Wagon Wheels
- June
Fish Quilt
- July
May Basket
Periwinkle
Quint Five
"H" Square
- August
Starry Heavens
Friendship Chain
Flowers in a Basket
Contrary Wife
- September
Star Spangled Banner
1941 Nine Patch
Quilt in Light and Dark
- October
Four Buds
Radio Windmill
Four Leaf Clover
- November
Buzz Saw
Star of Alamo
Winding Blade
Kitchen Woodbox
- December
Friendship Ring
Whirling Five Patch
Old Indian Trail
Mexican Star

1942
- January
Sunlight and Shadows
Ice Cream Cone
Arrowheads
Molly's Rose Garden
- February
Tulips
Postage Stamp
Chain Quilt
- March
Four O' Clock
- April
Long Pointed Star
Victory Quilt
Victory Quilt in Another Version
- May
Salute to the Colors
Ola's Quilt
Rosebud
Depression Quilt
- June
Airplane

- September
Ice Cream Cone
Whirling Pinwheel
Broken Wheel
- October
Fence Row
World Fair
- November
Lone Star
- December
Formal Flower Bed
Patchwork Cushion Top
Mowing Machine

1944
- January
Striped Plain Quilt
- February
Butterfly in Angles
Washington Stamp
- March
Whirling Blade
Jack in the Pulpit
Evening Star
- April
Friendship Name Chain
- May
Rosebud
President Roosevelt
New Four Pointer
- June
Sailboat Oklahoma
- July
Blue Blades Flying
- August
Soldier Boy
Seven Stars
Solomon's Puzzle
- September
Roads to Berlin
Envelope Quilt
Victory Boat
- October
Goose Track
- November
Hearts and Diamonds in
Applique
This and That
- December
Irish Chain

1945
- January
Gate or "H" Quilt
Oklahoma Star
- February
Diamonds and Arrow Points
- March

Hearts and Flowers

INDEX OF PATTERNS

Morning Sun
Southern Star
- April
Scottish Cross
- May
Friendship Quilt
Parallelogram Block
- June
Log Cabin
Grandmother's Cross
- July
Little Wedding Ring
Diversion Quilt
- August
Four Diamonds
Arkansas Traveler
Field Flower Applique
- September
Quilt Mosaic
Modern Envelope
- October
Baby Fan Applique
Circle in a Frame
- November
Small Triangle
Sailboat in Blue and White
Dove at the Window

1946
- February
Fenced-In Star
Cup and Saucer
- March
Simplicity's Delight
- April
Double Irish Chain
Wee Fan
Basket of Bright Flowers
- May
Basket
- July
Semi-Circle Saw
Meadow Rose
Steps to the Altar
- August
White Cross
May Basket for Applique
- October
Return of the Swallows
- November
Rose Dream
- December
Mother's Choice

1947
- January
Red Cross
- February

Springtime Blossoms
- March
Ratchet Wheel
- April
Airplane Motif
Little Boy's Britches
Pieced Sunflower
- June
Road to Oklahoma
Mystery Snowball
Hen and Her Chicks
Tulip Quilt
- July
Four-Leaf Clover
Wedding Ring
- August
Friendship Quilt
Cottage Tulips
- September
May Basket in Floral
Tones
Century-Old Tulip Pattern
- October
Frame with Diamonds
Compass Quilt
Builder's Blocks
- November
Carrie Nation
- December
Broken Star
Double "T"
Christmas Star

1948
- January
Steps to the Altar
Crazy Tile
4-Part Strip Block
- February
Circle Upon Circle
Stepping Stones
- March
Wagon Wheels
Boutonniere
- April
Spider Web
Liberty Star
Spring Beauty
- June
Spool Quilt
Royal Diamonds
- July
Double Irish Chain
Sea Shell
- August
Milkmaid's Star
Fans and a Ring
Thrifty Wife

- September
Pig Pen
Log Cabin
- October
Arkansas Star
Old Spanish Tile
- November
Grandmother's Quilt
Whirling Diamonds
- December
Three-In-One
Star Chain
Granny's Choice

1949
- January
Crown of Thorns
Betty's Delight
Tulip Pattern in High Colors
- February
Long Nine Patch
- March
Autograph Quilt
North Star
Lace Edge
- April
Flash of Diamonds
Terrapin
- May
Magnolia Bud
Kansas Star
- June
Crazy Anne
Chips and Whetstones
- September
Hollows and Squares
Bright Jewel
- October
Gay Dutch Tile
Greek Cross
Ducklings for Friendship
Arrowhead Star
- November
Pussy in the Corner

1950
- January
Broken Stone
- February
Love in a Tangle
Bleeding Heart
Missouri Morning Star
Queen Charlotte's Crown
- March
Snowball
- April
Grandma's Hopscotch
Triangles and Squares

- May
Jewel Quilt
Wishing Ring
- June
Oklahoma String
Scottie Quilt for Boys
- July
Whirligig
- August
Little Girl's Star
Yellow Square
- September
Rainbow Quilt
- October
Parquetry for a Quilt
Block
- November
Christmas Tree
Feather-Bone Block
- December
Spindles and Stripes

1951
- January
Little Wedding Ring
- February
Picture Frames
- March
Box of Tulips
Remnant Ovals
Star in a Square
Four Vases
- April
Heirloom Jewel
- May
Flower Garden
Mother's Choice
- June
Soldier Boy
- July
4-Square Block with Diamonds
Heart for Applique
- September
Panel of Roses
Whirling Windmill
- October
Block of Many Triangles
Name is Hesper
- December
Spool Quilt
Brave Sunflower

1952
- January
Winged Four-Patch
- March
Golden Wedding Ring
Pickle Dish

Other Kansas City Star Quilt books:

- Star Quilts I: One Piece at a Time
- Star Quilts II: More Kansas City Star Quilts
- Star Quilts III: Outside the Box
- Star Quilts IV: The Sister Blocks
- Star Quilts V: Prairie Flower — A Year on the Plains
- Star Quilts VI: Kansas City Quiltmakers
- Star Quilts VII: O'Glory — Americana Quilt Blocks from The Kansas City Star
- Santa's Parade of Nursery Rhymes
- Fan Quilt Memories

For more information or to order, call 816-234-4636 and say "Books."
Or visit www.PickleDish.com